The Public Library of Nashville and Davidson County

Night Must Fall

A PLAY IN THREE ACTS

By

EMLYN WILLIAMS

SAMUEL FRENCH, Inc.
25 West 45th Street, New York, N. Y.
811 West 7th Street, Los Angeles, Calif.
SAMUEL FRENCH. Ltd., London
SAMUEL FRENCH (Canada) Ltd., Toronto

"NIGHT MUST FALL"

ALL RIGHTS RESERVED

To
M. W.

STORY OF THE PLAY

Dan is a bellboy in a resort hotel remotely located in Essex, England. Having seduced Dora Parkoe, maid at Mrs. Bramson's, Dan is summoned to the Bramson cottage. Such is his charm that Mrs. Bramson is immediately taken with him, adding him to her household servants. The murder of a guest at the hotel is traced to Dan by Olivia, an unhappy niece of Mrs. Bramson's, who elects to shield the boy. Dan, grateful but powerless in the grip of his homicidal instincts, plots the murder of Mrs. Bramson for her money. The police take him away to be hanged, leaving Olivia relieved but desolate.

A drama in three acts by Emlyn Williams. Produced by Sam H. Harris at the Ethel Barrymore Theatre, New York.

CAST OF CHARACTERS

THE LORD CHIEF JUSTICE .... *Ben Webster*

MRS. BRAMSON .... *May Whitty*

OLIVIA GRAYNE .... *Angela Baddeley*

HUBERT LAURIE .... *Michael Shepley*

NURSE LIBBY .... *Shirley Gale*

MRS. TERENCE .... *Doris Hare*

DORA PARKOE .... *Betty Jardine*

INSPECTOR BELSIZE .... *Mathew Boulton*

DAN .... *Emlyn Williams*

BEFORE THE PLAY—*The Court of Criminal Appeal, London.*

ACTS I, II AND III—*Sitting Room of Forest Corner, Mrs. Bramson's Bungalow, Essex, England.*

DESCRIPTION OF CHARACTERS

LORD CHIEF JUSTICE: *Sitting in judgment, wearing wig and red robes of office, in the Court of Criminal Appeal.*

MRS. BRAMSON: *She is a fussy, discontented, common woman of fifty-five, old-fashioned both in clothes and coiffure.*

NURSE LIBBY: *A kindly, matter-of-fact young north-country woman in district nurse's uniform.*

OLIVIA GRAYNE: *She is a subdued young woman of twenty-eight, her hair tied severely in a knot, wearing horn-rimmed spectacles.*

HUBERT LAURIE: *He is thirty-five, moustached, hearty, and pompous.*

MRS. TERENCE: *She is the cook, middle-aged, Cockney, and fearless.*

DORA: *She is a pretty, stupid, and rather sluttish country girl of twenty, wearing a maid's uniform.*

BELSIZE: *He is an entirely inconspicuous man of fifty, dressed in tweeds: his suavity hides any amount of strength.*

DAN: *He is a young fellow wearing a blue pill-box hat, uniform trousers, a jacket too small for him, and bicycle-clips: the stub of a cigarette dangles between his lips. He speaks with a rough accent, indeterminate, but more Welsh than anything else. His personality varies very considerably as the play proceeds: the impression he gives at the moment is one of totally disarming good humour and childlike unself-consciousness. It would need a very close observer to suspect that there is something wrong somewhere—that this personality is completely assumed.*

THE CHARACTERS
(in the order of their appearance)

THE LORD CHIEF JUSTICE
MRS. BRAMSON
OLIVIA GRAYNE   Her niece
HUBERT LAURIE
NURSE LIBBY
MRS. TERENCE   Mrs. Bramson's cook
DORA PARKOE   Her maid
INSPECTOR BELSIZE
DAN

BEFORE THE PLAY
The Court of Criminal Appeal

The action of the play takes place in the sitting-room of Forest Corner, Mrs. Bramson's bungalow in Essex.

The time is the present.

ACT I
A morning in October.

ACT II
SCENE I: An afternoon twelve days later.
SCENE II: Late afternoon, two days later.

ACT III
SCENE I: Half an hour later. Nightfall.
SCENE II: Half an hour later.

BEFORE THE PLAY

The orchestra plays light tunes until the house lights are turned down; the curtain rises in darkness, accompanied by solemn music. A small light grows in the middle of the stage, and shows the LORD CHIEF JUSTICE *sitting in judgment, wearing wig and red robes of office, in the Court of Criminal Appeal. His voice, cold and disapproving, gradually swells up with the light as he reaches his peroration.*

LORD CHIEF JUSTICE : ... and there is no need to recapitulate here the arguments for and against this point of law, which we heard in the long and extremely fair summing up at the trial of the appellant at the Central Criminal Court. The case was clearly put to the jury; and it is against sentence of death for these two murders that the prisoner now appeals. Which means that the last stage of this important and extremely horrible case has now been reached. On a later page in the summing up, the learned judge said this ... *(turning over papers)* ... "This case has, through the demeanour of the prisoner in the witness-box, obtained the most widespread and scandalous publicity, which I would beg you most earnestly, members of the jury, to

11

forget." I cannot help thinking that the deplorable atmosphere of sentimental melodrama which has pervaded this trial has made the *theatre* a more fitting background for it than a court of law; but we are in a court of law, nevertheless, and the facts have been placed before the court. A remarkable and in my opinion praiseworthy feature of the case has been that the *sanity* of the prisoner has never been called into question; and, like the learned judge, the Court must dismiss as mischievous pretence the attitude of this young man who stands convicted of two brutal murders in cold blood. This case has, from beginning to end, exhibited no feature calling for sympathy; the evidence has on every point been conclusive, and on this evidence the jury have convicted the appellant. In the opinion of the Court there is no reason to interfere with that conviction, and this appeal must be dismissed.

The chords of solemn music are heard again, and the stage gradually darkens. A few seconds later the music merges into the sound of church bells playing far away, and the lights come up on.

ACT I

The sitting-room of Forest Corner, MRS. BRAM-
SON's *bungalow in a forest in Essex. A fine morning in October.*

Centre back, a small hall; in its left side the
front door of the house (throughout the play,
"left" and "right" refer to the audience's left
and right). Thick plush curtains can be drawn
across the entrance to the hall; they are open at
the moment. Windows, one on each side of the
hall, with window-seats and net curtains beyond
which can be glimpsed the pine-trees of the forest. In the left wall, upstage, a door leading to
the kitchen. In the left wall, downstage, the fireplace; above it, a cretonne-covered sofa, next to
a very solid cupboard built into the wall; below
it a cane armchair. In the right wall, upstage, a
door leading to MRS. BRAMSON's bedroom. In the
right wall, downstage, wide-open paned doors
leading to the sun-room. Right downstage, next
the sun-room, a large dining-table with four
straight chairs round it. Between the bedroom
and the sun-room, a desk with books on it, a cupboard below it, and a hanging mirror on the
wall above. Above the bedroom, a corner medi-

15

cine cupboard. Between the hall and the right window, an occasional table.

The bungalow is tawdry but cheerful; it is built entirely of wood, with an oil lamp fixed in the wall over the occasional table. The room is comfortably furnished, though in fussy and eccentric Victorian taste; stuffed birds, Highland cattle in oils, antimacassars, and wax fruit are unobtrusively in evidence. On the mantelpiece, an ornate chiming clock. The remains of breakfast on a tray on the table.

MRS. BRAMSON *is sitting in a wheeled chair in the centre of the room. She is a fussy, discontented, common woman of fifty-five, old-fashioned both in clothes and coiffure;* NURSE LIBBY, *a kindly, matter-of-fact young north-country woman in district nurse's uniform, is sitting on the sofa, massaging one of her hands.* OLIVIA GRAYNE *sits on the old woman's right; holding a book; she is a subdued young woman of twenty-eight, her hair tied severely in a knot, wearing horn-rimmed spectacles; there is nothing in any way remarkable about her at the moment.* HUBERT LAURIE *is sitting in the armchair, scanning the "Daily Telegraph." He is thirty-five, moustached, hearty, and pompous, wearing plus fours and smoking a pipe.*

A pause. The church bells die away.

MRS. BRAMSON (*sharply*): Go on.

OLIVIA (*reading*): "...Lady Isabel humbly crossed her attenuated hands upon her chest. 'I am on my way to God,' she whispered, 'to an-

16

swer for all my sins and sorrows.' 'Child,' said Miss Carlyle, 'had *I* anything to do with sending you from...' (*turning over*) '...East Lynne?' Lady Isabel shook her head and cast down her gaze."

MRS. BRAMSON (*aggressively*): Now that's what **I** call a beautiful character.

NURSE: Very pretty. But the poor thing'd have felt that much better tucked up in 'ospital instead of lying about her own home gassing her 'ead off——

MRS. BRAMSON: Sh!

NURSE: Sorry.

OLIVIA (*reading*): "'Thank God,' inwardly breathed Miss Corny.... 'Forgive me,' she said loudly and in agitation. 'I want to see Archibald,' whispered Lady Isabel."

MRS. BRAMSON: You don't see many books like *East Lynne* about nowadays.

HUBERT: No, you don't.

OLIVIA (*reading*): "'I want to see Archibald,' whispered Lady Isabel. 'I have prayed Joyce to bring him to me, and she will not——'"

MRS. BRAMSON (*sharply*): Olivia!

OLIVIA: Yes, auntie?

MRS. BRAMSON (*craftily*): You're not skipping, are you?

OLIVIA: Am I?

MRS. BRAMSON: You've missed out about Lady Isabel taking up her cross and the weight of it killing her. I may be a fool, but I do know *East Lynne*.

OLIVIA : Perhaps there were two pages stuck together.

MRS. BRAMSON : Very convenient when you want your walk, eh? Yes, I *am* a fool, I suppose, as well as an invalid.

OLIVIA : But I thought you were so much better——

NURSE : You'd two helpings of bacon at breakfast, remember——

MRS. BRAMSON : Doctor's orders. You know every mouthful's agony to me.

HUBERT (*deep in his paper*) : There's a man here in Weston-super-Mare who stood on his head for twenty minutes for a bet, and he hasn't come to yet.

MRS. BRAMSON (*sharply*) : I thought this morning I'd never be able to face the day.

HUBERT : But last night when you opened the port——

MRS. BRAMSON : I've had a relapse since then. My heart's going like anything. Give me a chocolate.

OLIVIA *rises and fetches her a chocolate from a large box on the table.*

NURSE : How does it feel?

MRS. BRAMSON : Nasty. (*Munching her chocolate.*) I *know* it's neuritis.

NURSE : You know, Mrs. Bramson, what you want isn't massage at all, only exercise. Your body——

MRS. BRAMSON : Don't you dictate to me about my body. Nobody here understands my body or anything else about me. As for sympathy, I've

forgotten the meaning of the word. (*To* OLIVIA)
What's the matter with your face?

OLIVIA (*startled*): I—I really don't know.

MRS. BRAMSON: It's as long as my arm.

OLIVIA (*drily*): I'm afraid it's made like that.
She crosses the room, and comes back again.

MRS. BRAMSON: What are you walking up and
down for? What's the matter with you? Aren't
you happy here?

OLIVIA: It's a bit lonely, but I'll get used to it.

MRS. BRAMSON: Lonely? All these lovely woods?
What are you talking about? Don't you like na
ture?

NURSE: Will that be all for to-day?

MRS. BRAMSON: I suppose it'll have to be.

NURSE (*rising and taking her bag from the sofa*):
Well, I've that confined lady still waiting in
Shepperley. (*Going into the hall*) Toodle-oo!

MRS. BRAMSON: Mind you call again Wednesday.
In case my neuritis sets in again.

NURSE (*turning in the hall*): I will that. And if
paralysis pops up, let me know. Toodle-oo!
She marches cheerily out of the front door.
MRS. BRAMSON *cannot make up her mind if the
last remark is sarcastic or not. She concentrates
on* OLIVIA.

MRS. BRAMSON: You know, you mustn't think
just because this house is lonely you're going to
get a rise in salary. Oh, no....I expect you've
an idea I'm worth a good bit of money, haven't
you?...It isn't my money you're after, is it?

OLIVIA (*setting chairs to rights round the table*):

I'm sorry, but my sense of humour can't stand the strain. I'll have to go.

MRS. BRAMSON: Can you afford to go?

OLIVIA (*after a pause, controlling herself*): You know I can't.

MRS. BRAMSON: Then don't talk such nonsense. Clear the breakfast things.

OLIVIA *hesitates, then crosses to the kitchen door.*

(*Muttering*): Sense of humour indeed, never heard of such a thing. . . .

OLIVIA (*at the door*): Mrs. Terence, will you clear away?

She goes to the left window, and looks out.

MRS. BRAMSON: You wait, my girl. Pride comes before a fall. Won't catch a husband with your nose in the air, you know.

OLIVIA: I don't want a husband.

MRS. BRAMSON: Don't like men, I suppose? Never heard of them, I suppose? Don't believe you. See?

OLIVIA (*resigned*): I see. It's going to be a fine day.

MRS. BRAMSON (*taking up "East Lynne" from the table*): It'll cloud over, I expect.

OLIVIA: I don't think so. The trees look beautiful with the sun on them. Everything looks so clean. (*Lifting up three books from the window seat*) Shall I pack the other half of Mrs. Henry Wood?

MRS. BRAMSON: Mrs. Henry Wood? Who's Mrs. Henry Wood? Pack the other half of Mrs.

Henry Wood? What *are* you talking about?

OLIVIA: She wrote your favourite book—*East Lynne.*

MRS. BRAMSON (*looking at her book*): Oh... (*Picking a paper out of it.*) What's this? (*Reading ponderously*) A sonnet. "The flame of passion is not red but white, not quick but slow——"

OLIVIA (*going to her and snatching it from her with a cry*): Don't!

MRS. BRAMSON: Writing *poetry!* That's a hobby and a half, I must say! "Flame of passion..." *well!*

OLIVIA (*crossing to the fireplace*): It's only a silly poem I amused myself with at college. It's not meant for anybody but me.

MRS. BRAMSON: You're a dark horse, you are.

MRS. TERENCE *enters from the kitchen. She is the cook, middle-aged, Cockney, and fearless. She carries a bunch of roses.*

MRS. TERENCE (*grimly*): Would you be wanting anything?

MRS. BRAMSON: Yes. Clear away.

MRS. TERENCE: That's Dora's job. Where's Dora?

OLIVIA: She's gone into the clearing for some firewood.

MRS. BRAMSON: You can't expect the girl to gather firewood with one hand and clear breakfast with the other. Clear away.

MRS. TERENCE (*crossing to the table, under her breath*): All right, you sour-faced old hag.

HUBERT *drops his pipe.* MRS. BRAMSON *winces*

21

and looks away. MRS. TERENCE *clears the table.*

HUBERT (*to* OLIVIA): What—what was that she said?

MRS. TERENCE: She 'eard. And then she 'as to save 'er face and pretend she 'asn't. She knows nobody but me'd stay with 'er a day if I went.

MRS. BRAMSON: She oughtn't to talk to me like that. I know she steals my sugar.

MRS. TERENCE: That's a living lie. (*Going round to her*) Here are your roses.

MRS. BRAMSON: You've cut them too young. I knew you would.

MRS. TERENCE (*taking up her tray and starting for the kitchen*): Then you come out and pick the ones you want, and you'll only 'ave yourself to blame.

MRS. BRAMSON: That's a nice way to talk to an invalid.

MRS. TERENCE: If you're an invalid, I'm the Prince of Wales.

She goes back into the kitchen.

OLIVIA: Would you like me to read some more?

BRAMSON: No. I'm upset for the day now. I'd better see she does pick the right roses. (*Wheeling herself, muttering*) That woman's a menace. Good mind to bring an action against her. She ought to be put away.... (*Shouting*) Wait for me, wait for me!

Her voice dies away in the kitchen. The kitchen door closes. HUBERT *and* OLIVIA *are alone.*

OLIVIA: That's the fifth action she's threatened

to bring this week. (*She crosses to the right window.*)

HUBERT: She's a good one to talk about putting away. Crikey! She'll be found murdered one of these days.... (*Suddenly reading from his paper*) "In India a population of three and a half hundred million is loyal to Britain; now——"

OLIVIA: Oh, Hubert! (*Good humouredly*) I thought I'd cured you of that.

HUBERT: Sorry.

OLIVIA: You've only had two weeks of her. I've had six.

A pause. She sighs restlessly.

HUBERT: Fed up?

OLIVIA: It's such a very inadequate expression, don't you think?... (*After a pause*) How bright the sun is to-day....

She is pensive, far-away, smiling.

HUBERT: A penny for 'em.

OLIVIA: I was just thinking...I often wonder on a very fine morning what it'll be like... for night to come. And I never can. And yet it's got to.... (*Looking at his perplexed face*) It *is* silly, isn't it?

DORA comes in from the kitchen with a duster and crosses towards the bedroom. She is a pretty, stupid, and rather sluttish country girl of twenty, wearing a maid's uniform. She looks depressed.

Who are those men, Dora?

DORA: What men, miss?

23

OLIVIA: Over there, behind the clearing.

DORA: Oh.... (*Peering past her*) Oh. 'Adn't seen them. What are they doing poking about in that bush?

OLIVIA (*absently*): I don't know. I saw them yesterday too, farther down the woods.

DORA (*lamely*): I expect they're looking for something.

She goes into the bedroom.

HUBERT: She looks a bit off-colour, doesn't she?

OLIVIA: The atmosphere must be getting her down too.

HUBERT: I'm wondering if I'm going to be able to stand it myself. Coming over here every day for another week.

OLIVIA (*smiling*): There's nothing to prevent you staying at *home* every day for another week ...is there?

HUBERT (*still apparently reading his paper*): Oh, yes, there is. What d'you think I invite myself to lunch every day for? You don't think it's the old geyser, do you?

OLIVIA (*smiling*): No.

She comes down to the table.

HUBERT: Don't want to sound rude, et cetera, but women don't get men proposing to them every day, you know... (*Turning over a page*) Gosh, what a wizard machine——

OLIVIA (*sitting at the left of the table*): I can't think *why* you want to marry me, as a matter of fact. It isn't the same as if I were very pretty, or something.

HUBERT: You do say some jolly rum things, Olivia, upon my soul.

OLIVIA: *I'll* tell *you* why, then, if it makes you feel any better. You're cautious; and you want to marry me because I'm quiet. I'd make you a steady wife, and run a home for you.

HUBERT: There's nothing to be ashamed of in being steady. I'm steady myself.

OLIVIA: I know you are.

HUBERT: Then why aren't you keen?

OLIVIA (*after a pause, tolerant but weary*): Because you're an unmitigated bore.

HUBERT: A bore? (*Horrified*) *Me*, a bore? Upon my word, Olivia, I think you're a bit eccentric, I do really. Sorry to be rude, and all that, but that's put the kybosh on it! People could call me a thing or two, but I've never been called a bore!

OLIVIA: Bores never are. People are too bored with them to call them anything.

HUBERT: I suppose you'd be more likely to say "Yes" if I were an unmitigated bounder?

OLIVIA (*with a laugh*): Oh, don't be silly....

HUBERT (*going to her*): You're a rum girl, Olivia, upon my soul you are. P'raps that's why I think you're so jolly attractive. Like a mouse one minute, and then this straight-from-the-shoulder business.... What *is* a sonnet?

OLIVIA: It's a poem of fourteen lines.

HUBERT: Oh, yes, Shakespeare.... Never knew you did a spot of rhyming, Olivia! Now that's what I mean about you.... We'll have to start calling you Elizabeth Brontë!

She turns away. He studies her.

You *are* bored, aren't you?

He walks to the sun-room. She rouses herself and turns to him impetuously.

OLIVIA: I'm being silly, I know—of course I *ought* to get married, and *of course* this is a wonderful chance, and——

HUBERT (*moving to her*): Good egg! Then you will?

OLIVIA (*stalling*): Give me a—another week or two—will you?

HUBERT: Oh. My holiday's up on the twenty-seventh.

OLIVIA: I know I'm being tiresome, but——

MRS. BRAMSON (*in the kitchen*): The most disgraceful thing I've ever heard——

HUBERT: She's coming back....

OLIVIA *rises and goes to the right window.* HUBERT *hurries into the sun-room.* MRS. BRAMSON *is wheeled back from the kitchen by* MRS. TERENCE, *to the centre of the room. She* (MRS. BRAMSON) *has found the pretext for the scene she has been longing to make since she got up this morning.*

MRS. BRAMSON: Fetch that girl here. This minute.

MRS. TERENCE: Oh, leave the child alone.

MRS. BRAMSON: Leave her alone, the little sneak-thief? Fetch her here.

MRS. TERENCE (*at the top of her voice*): Dora!

(*Opening the front door and calling into the trees*) Dora!

OLIVIA: What's Dora done now?

MRS. BRAMSON: Broken three of my Crown Derby, that's all. Thought if she planted them in the rose-bed I wouldn't be well enough ever to see them, I suppose. Well, I *have* seen.

MRS. TERENCE (*crossing and calling to the bedroom*): You're wanted.

DORA'S VOICE: What for?

MRS. TERENCE: She wants to kiss you good morning, what d'you think....

She collects the table-cloth, fetches a vase from the mantelpiece, and goes into the kitchen. DORA *enters gingerly from the bedroom, carrying a cup and saucer on a tray.*

DORA: Did you want me, mum?

MRS. BRAMSON: Crown Derby to you, my girl.

DORA (*uncertain*): Beg pardon, mum?

MRS. BRAMSON: I suppose you think that china came from Marks and Spencer?

DORA: Oh.... (*Snivelling*) Oh...oh...

OLIVIA (*coming between* DORA *and* MRS. BRAMSON): Come along, Dora, it's not as bad as all that.

DORA: Oh, yes, it is....Oh....

MRS. BRAMSON: You can leave, that's all. You can leave.

Appalled, DORA *drops the tray and breaks the saucer.*

That settles it. Now you'll *have* to leave.

DORA (*with a cry*): Oh, please I... (*Kneeling,*

and collecting broken china) Oh, ma'am—I'm not meself, you see.... (*Snivelling*) I'm in—terrible trouble....

MRS. BRAMSON : Have you been stealing?

DORA (*shocked*): Oh, no!

OLIVIA (*after a pause*): Are you going to have a baby?

After a pause, DORA *nods.*

DORA (*putting the china in her apron*): The idea of me stealing.... I do go to Sunday school, anyways....

MRS. BRAMSON : So that's the game. Wouldn't think butter would melt in her mouth.... You'll have to go, of course ; I can't have that sort of thing in this house—and stop squeaking! You'll bring my heart on again. It's all this modern life. I've always said so. All these films and rubbish.

OLIVIA : My dear auntie, you can't have a baby by just sitting in the pictures.

MRS. BRAMSON : Go away, and don't interfere.

OLIVIA *goes to the left window.* DORA *rises.*

(*Triumphantly*) So you're going to have a child. When?

DORA (*sniffling*): Last August Bank Holiday....

MRS. BRAMSON : What?...Oh!

DORA : I 'aven't got a penny only what I earn —and if I lose my job 'ere——

MRS. BRAMSON : He'll have to marry you.

DORA : Oh, I don't think he's keen....

MRS. BRAMSON : I'll *make* him keen. Who is the gentleman?

DORA: A boy I know; Dan his name is—'leas'
'e's not a gentleman. He's a page-boy at the
Tallboys.

MRS. BRAMSON: The Tallboys? D'you mean that
new-fangled place all awnings and loud speakers
and things?

DORA: That's right. On the by-pass.

MRS. BRAMSON: Just the nice ripe sort of place
for mischief, it always looked to me. All those
lanterns.... What's his character, the good-for-
nothing scoundrel?

DORA: Oh, he's nice, really. He done the wrong
thing by me, but he's all right, if you know
what I mean....

MRS BRAMSON: No, I don't. Where does he come
from?

DORA: He's sort of Welsh, I think. 'E's been to
sea, too. He's funny, of course. Ever so open.
Baby-face they call him. Though I never seem
to get 'old of what 'e's thinking, somehow——

MRS. BRAMSON: I'll get hold of what he's thinking, all right. I've had my knife into that sort
ever since I was a girl.

DORA: Oh, mum, if I got him to let you speak
to him—d'you think I could stay on?

MRS. BRAMSON (*after a pause*): *If* he marries you
at once.

DORA: Shall I—— (*Eagerly*) As a matter of fact,
ma'am, he's gone on a message on his bicycle to
Payley Hill this morning, and he said he might
pop in to see me on the way back——

MRS. BRAMSON: That's right; nothing like visitors to brighten your mornings, eh? I'll deal with him.

DORA: Yes.... (*Going, and turning at the kitchen door—in impulsive relief*) Oh, ma'am——

MRS. BRAMSON: And I'll stop the Crown Derby out of your wages.

DORA (*crestfallen*): Oh!

MRS. BRAMSON: What were you going to say?

DORA: Well, ma'am, I *was* going to say I don't know how to thank you for your generosity....

She goes into the kitchen. The clock chimes.

MRS. BRAMSON: Olivia!

OLIVIA: Yes, auntie?

MRS. BRAMSON: You've forgotten again. Medicine's overdue. Most important.

OLIVIA crosses to the medicine cupboard and fetches the medicine. MRS. TERENCE comes in from the kitchen with a vase of flowers and barges between the sofa and the wheelchair.

MRS. TERENCE (*muttering*): All this furniture...

MRS. BRAMSON (*to her*): Did *you* know she's having a baby?

MRS. TERENCE (*coldly*): She did mention it in conversation.

MRS. BRAMSON: Playing with fire, that's the game nowadays.

MRS. TERENCE (*arranging flowers as* OLIVIA *gives* MRS. BRAMSON *her medicine*): Playing with fiddlesticks. We're only young once; that 'ot summer too. She's been a fool, but she's no criminal. And, talking of criminals, there's a p'liceman at the kitchen door.

MRS. BRAMSON : A what?

MRS. TERENCE : A p'liceman. A bobby.

MRS. BRAMSON : What does he want?

MRS. TERENCE : Better ask 'im. I know *my* conscience is clear; I don't know about other people's.

MRS. BRAMSON : But I've never had a policeman
coming to see me before!

DORA *runs in from the kitchen.*

DORA (*terrified*): There's a man there! From the
p'lice! 'E said something about the Tallboys!
'E—'e 'asn't come about me, 'as 'e?

MRS. TERENCE : Of course he 'asn't——

MRS. BRAMSON : He may have.

MRS. TERENCE : Don't frighten the girl; she's simple enough now.

MRS. BRAMSON (*sharply*): It's against the law,
what she's done, isn't it? (*To* DORA) Go back in
there till he sends for you.

DORA *creeps back into the kitchen.*

OLIVIA (*at the left window*): He isn't a policeman, as a matter of fact. He must be a plain-
clothes man.

MRS. TERENCE (*sardonically*): Scotland Yard, I
should think.

BELSIZE *is seen outside, crossing the left window
to the front door.*

MRS. BRAMSON : That place in those detective
books? Don't be so silly.

MRS. TERENCE : He says he wants to see you very
particular——

A sharp rat-tat at the front door.

31

(*Going to the hall*) On a very particular matter. . . .

(*Turning on* MRS. BRAMSON) And don't you start
callin' *me* silly !

Going to the front door, and opening it.
This way, sir. . . .

BELSIZE *enters, followed by* MRS. TERENCE. *He
is an entirely inconspicuous man of fifty, dressed
in tweeds : his suavity hides any amount of
strength.*

BELSIZE : Mrs. Bramson ? I'm sorry to break in
on you like this. My card. . . .

MRS. BRAMSON (*taking it, sarcastically*) : I suppose
you're going to tell me you're from Scotland
Ya—— (*She sees the name on the card.*)

BELSIZE : I see you've all your wits about you !

MRS. BRAMSON : Oh. (*Reading incredulously*)
Criminal Investigation Department !

BELSIZE (*smiling*) : A purely informal visit, I
assure you.

MRS. BRAMSON : I don't like having people in my
house that I don't know.

BELSIZE (*the velvet glove*) : I'm afraid the law
sometimes makes it necessary.

MRS. TERENCE *gives him a chair next the table.
He sits.* MRS. TERENCE *stands behind the table.*

MRS. BRAMSON (*to her*) : You can go.

MRS. TERENCE : I don't want to go. I might 'ave
to be arrested for stealing sugar.

BELSIZE : Sugar ? . . . As a matter of fact, you
might be useful. Any of you may be useful.
Mind my pipe ?

MRS. BRAMSON *blows in disgust and waves her hand before her face.*

MRS. BRAMSON : Is it about my maid having an illegitimate child?

BELSIZE : I beg your pardon?... Oh no! That sort of thing's hardly in my line, thank God... Lonely spot... (*To* MRS. TERENCE) Long way for you to walk every day, isn't it?

MRS. TERENCE : I don't walk. I cycle.

BELSIZE : Oh.

MRS. BRAMSON : What's the matter?

BELSIZE : I just thought if she walked she might use some of the paths, and have seen—something.

MRS. BRAMSON ⎱ Something of what?
MRS. TERENCE ⎰ Something?

BELSIZE : I'll tell you. I——

A piano is heard in the sun-room, playing the "Merry Widow" waltz.

(*Casually*) Other people in the house?

MRS. BRAMSON (*calling shrilly*) : Mr. Laurie!

The piano stops.

HUBERT'S VOICE (*as the piano stops, in the sun-room*) : Yes?

MRS. BRAMSON (*to* OLIVIA, *sourly*) : Did *you* ask him to play the piano?

HUBERT *comes back from the sun-room.*

HUBERT (*breezily*) : Hello, house on fire or something?

MRS. BRAMSON : Very nearly. This is Mr.—er— Bel——

BELSIZE : Belsize.

MRS. BRAMSON (*drily*) : Of Scotland Yard.

HUBERT: Oh.... (*Apprehensive*) It isn't about my car, is it?

BELSIZE: No.

HUBERT: Oh. (*Shaking hands affably*) How do you do?

BELSIZE: How do you do, sir....

MRS. BRAMSON: He's a friend of Miss Grayne's here. Keeps calling.

BELSIZE: Been calling long?

MRS. BRAMSON: Every day for two weeks. Just before lunch.

HUBERT: Well——

OLIVIA (*sitting on the sofa*): Perhaps I'd better introduce myself. I'm Olivia Grayne, Mrs. Bramson's niece. I work for her.

BELSIZE: Oh, I see. Thanks. Well now...

HUBERT (*sitting at the table, effusively*): I know a chap on the Stock Exchange who was taken last year and shown over the Black Museum at Scotland Yard.

BELSIZE (*politely*): Really——

MRS. BRAMSON: And what d'you expect the policeman to do about it?

HUBERT: Well, it was very interesting, he said. Bit ghoulish, of course——

BELSIZE: I expect so.... (*Getting down to business*) Now I wonder if any of you've seen anything in the least out of the ordinary round here lately? Anybody called—anybody strange wandering about in the woods—overheard anything?

They look at one another.

MRS. BRAMSON : The only visitor's been the doctor—and the district nurse.

MRS. TERENCE : Been ever so gay.

HUBERT : As a matter of fact, funny thing did happen to me. Tuesday afternoon it was, I remember now.

BELSIZE : Oh ?

HUBERT (*graphically*) : I was walking back to my cottage from golf, and I heard something moving stealthily behind a tree, or a bush, or something.

BELSIZE (*interested*) : Oh, yes ?

HUBERT : Turned out to be a squirrel.

MRS. BRAMSON (*in disgust*) : Oh ! ...

HUBERT : No bigger than my hand ! Funny thing to happen, I thought.

BELSIZE : Very funny. Anything else ?

HUBERT : Not a thing. By Jove, fancy walking in the woods and stumbling over a dead body ! Most embarrassing !

MRS. TERENCE : I've stumbled over bodies in them woods afore now. But they wasn't dead. Oh, no.

MRS. BRAMSON : Say what you know, and don't talk so much.

MRS. TERENCE : Well, I've told 'im all I've seen. A bit o' love now and again. Though 'ow they make do with all them pine-needles beats me.

BELSIZE : Anything else ?

MRS. BRAMSON : Miss Grayne's always moping round the woods. Perhaps *she* can tell you something.

OLIVIA : I haven't seen anything, I'm afraid. . . . Oh—I saw some men beating the undergrowth—

BELSIZE : Yes, I'm coming to that. But no tramps, for instance ?

OLIVIA : N-no, I don't think so.

HUBERT : "Always carry a stick's" my motto. I'd like to see a tramp try anything on with me. Ah-ha ! Swish !

MRS. BRAMSON : What's all the fuss about ? Has there been a robbery or something ?

BELSIZE : There's a lady missing.

MRS. TERENCE : Where from ?

BELSIZE : The Tallboys.

MRS. BRAMSON : That Tallboys again——

BELSIZE : A Mrs. Chalfont.

MRS. TERENCE : Chalfont ? Oh, yes ! Dyed platinum blonde—widow of a colonel, so she says, livin' alone, so she says, always wearin' them faldalaldy openwork stockings. Fond of a drop too. That's 'er.

HUBERT : Why, d'you know her?

MRS. TERENCE : Never set eyes on 'er. But you know how people talk. Partial to that there, too, I'm told.

MRS. BRAMSON : What's that there ?

MRS. TERENCE : Ask me no questions, I'll tell you no lies.

BELSIZE (*quickly*) : Well, anyway . . . Mrs. Chalfont left the Tallboys last Friday afternoon, without a hat, went for a walk through the woods in this direction, and has never been seen since.

He makes his effect.

MRS. BRAMSON : I expect she was so drunk she fell flat and never came to.

BELSIZE : We've had the woods pretty well thrashed. (*To* OLIVIA) Those would be the men you saw. Now she was...

HUBERT (*taking the floor*): She may have had a brain-storm, you know, and taken a train somewhere. That's not uncommon, you know, among people of her sort. (*Airing knowledge*) And if what we gather from our friend here's true—and she's both a dipsomaniac *and* a nymphomaniac—

MRS. BRAMSON : Hark at the walking dictionary !

BELSIZE : We found her bag in her room ; and maniacs can't get far without cash...however dipso or nympho they may be....

HUBERT : Oh.

BELSIZE : She was a very flashy type of wo—she *is* a flashy type, I should say. At least I hope I should say...

MRS. BRAMSON : What d'you mean ? Why d'you hope ?

BELSIZE : Well...

OLIVIA : You don't mean she may be...she mayn't be alive ?

BELSIZE : It's possible.

MRS. BRAMSON : You'll be saying she's been murdered next !

BELSIZE : That's been known.

MRS. BRAMSON : Lot of stuff and nonsense. From a policeman too. Anybody'd think you'd been brought up on penny dreadfuls.

OLIVIA *turns and goes to the window.*

BELSIZE (*to* MRS. BRAMSON): Did you see about the fellow being hanged for the Ipswich murder? In last night's papers?

MRS. BRAMSON: I've lived long enough not to believe the papers.

BELSIZE: They occasionally print facts. And murder's occasionally a fact.

HUBERT: Everybody likes a good murder, as the saying goes! Remember those trials in the *Evening Standard* last year? Jolly interesting. I followed——

BELSIZE (*rising*): I'd be very grateful if you'd all keep your eyes and ears open, just in case ... (*Shaking hands*) Good morning ... good morning ... good morning, Mrs. Bramson. I must apologise again for intruding——

He turns to OLIVIA, *who is still looking out of the window.*

Good morning, Miss ... er ...

A pause.

OLIVIA (*starting*): I'm so sorry.

BELSIZE: Had you remembered something?

OLIVIA: Oh, no....

MRS. BRAMSON: What were you thinking, then?

OLIVIA: Only how ... strange it is.

BELSIZE: What?

OLIVIA: Well, here we all are, perfectly ordinary English people. We woke up ... no, it's silly.

MRS. BRAMSON: Of course it's silly.

BELSIZE (*giving* MRS. BRAMSON *an impatient look*): No, go on.

OLIVIA: Well, we woke up this morning, thinking, "Here's another day." We got up, looked at the weather, and talked; and here we all are, still talking.... And all that time——

MRS. BRAMSON: My dear girl, who are you to expect a policeman——

BELSIZE (*quelling her sternly*): If you please! I want to hear what she's got to say. (*To* OLIVIA) Well?

OLIVIA: All that time...there may be something...lying in the woods. Hidden under a bush, with two feet just showing. Perhaps one high heel catching the sunlight, with a bird perched on the end of it; and the other—a stockinged foot, with blood...that's dried into the openwork stocking. And there's a man walking about somewhere, and talking, like us; and he woke up this morning, and looked at the weather. ...And he killed her.... (*Smiling, looking out of the window*) The cat doesn't believe a word of it, anyhow. It's just walking away.

MRS. BRAMSON: Well!

MRS. TERENCE: Ooh, Miss Grayne, you give me the creeps! I'm glad it *is* morning, that's all I can say....

BELSIZE: I don't think the lady can quite describe *herself* as ordinary, after that little flight of fancy!

MRS. BRAMSON: Oh, that's nothing; she writes poetry. Jingle jingle——

BELSIZE: I can only hope she's wrong, or it'll mean a nice job of work for us!... Well, if anything funny happens, nip along to Shepperley police station. Pity you're not on the 'phone. Good morning.... Good morning....

MRS. TERENCE: This way....

She follows BELSIZE *into the hall.*

BELSIZE: No, don't bother.... Good morning.

He goes out. MRS. TERENCE *shuts the door after him.*

MRS. BRAMSON (*to* HUBERT): What are *you* staring at?

HUBERT (*crossing to the fireplace*): Funny, I can't get out of my mind what Olivia said about the man being somewhere who's done it.

MRS. TERENCE (*coming into the room*): Why, Mr. Laurie, it might be you! After all, there's nothing in your face that *proves* it isn't!

HUBERT: Oh, come, come! You're being a bit hard on the old countenance, aren't you?

MRS. TERENCE: Well, 'e's not going to walk about with bloodshot eyes and a snarl all over his face, is he?

She goes into the kitchen.

HUBERT: That's true enough.

MRS. BRAMSON: Missing woman indeed! She's more likely than not at this very moment sitting in some saloon bar. Or the films, I shouldn't wonder. (*To* OLIVIA) pass me my wool, will you....

OLIVIA *crosses to the desk. A knock at the kitchen door:* DORA *appears, cautiously.*

DORA: *Was* it about me?

OLIVIA: Of course it wasn't.

DORA (*relieved*): Oh.... Please, mum, 'e's 'ere.

MRS. BRAMSON: Who?

DORA: My boy fr—my gentleman friend, ma'am, from the Tallboys.

MRS. BRAMSON: I'm ready for him. (*Waving aside the wool which* OLIVIA *brings to her*) The sooner he's made to realise what his duty is, the better. *I*'ll give him baby-face!

DORA: Thank you, ma'am.

She goes out through the front door.

HUBERT: What gentleman? What duty?

OLIVIA: The maid's going to have a baby. (*She crosses and puts the wool in the cupboard of the desk.*)

HUBERT: Is she, by Jove!... Don't look at me like that, Mrs. Bramson! I've only been in the county two weeks.... But is *he* from the Tallboys?

MRS. BRAMSON: A page-boy or something of the sort.

DORA *comes back to the front door, looks back, and beckons. She is followed by* DAN, *who saunters past her into the room. He is a young fellow wearing a blue pill-box hat, uniform trousers, a jacket too small for him, and bicycle-clips: the stub of a cigarette dangles between his lips. He speaks with a rough accent, indeterminate, but more Welsh than anything else.*

His personality varies very considerably as the play proceeds: the impression he gives at the moment is one of totally disarming good humour and childlike unself-consciousness. It would need a very close observer to suspect that there is something wrong somewhere—that this personality is completely assumed. DORA *shuts the front door and comes to the back of the sofa.*

MRS. BRAMSON (*sternly*) : Well?

DAN (*saluting*) : Mornin', all!

MRS. BRAMSON : So you're Baby-face?

DAN : That's me. (*Grinning.*) Silly name, isn't it? (*After a pause.*) I must apologise to all and sundry for this fancy dress, but it's my working togs. I been on duty this mornin', and my hands isn't very clean. You see, I didn't know as it was going to be a party.

MRS. BRAMSON : Party?

DAN (*looking at* OLIVIA) : Well, it's ladies, isn't it?

HUBERT : Are you shy with ladies?

DAN (*smiling at* OLIVIA) : Oh, yes.

OLIVIA *moves away coldly.* DAN *turns to* MRS. BRAMSON.

MRS. BRAMSON (*cutting*) : You smoke, I see.

DAN : Yes. (*Taking the stub out of his mouth with alacrity and taking off his hat*) Oh, I'm sorry. I always forget my manners with a ciga-rette when I'm in company.... (*Pushing the stub behind his ear, as* OLIVIA *crosses to the armchair*) I always been clumsy in people's houses. I am sorry.

MRS. BRAMSON: You know my maid, Dora Parkoe, I believe?

DAN : Well, we have met, yes... (*with a grin at* DORA).

MRS. BRAMSON (*to* DORA) : Go away!

DORA *creeps back into the kitchen.*

You walked out with her last August Bank Holiday?

DAN : Yes....Excuse me smiling, but it sounds funny when you put it like that, doesn't it?

MRS. BRAMSON : You ought to be ashamed of yourself.

DAN (*soberly*) : Oh, I am.

MRS. BRAMSON : How did it happen?

DAN (*embarrassed*) : Well...we went...did *you* have a nice bank holiday?

MRS. BRAMSON : Answer my question!

HUBERT : Were you in love with the wench?

DAN : Oh, yes!

MRS. BRAMSON (*triumphantly*) : *When* did you first meet her?

DAN : Er—bank holiday morning.

MRS. BRAMSON : Picked her up, I suppose?

DAN : Oh, no, I didn't pick her up! I asked her for a match, and then I took her for a bit of a walk, to take her mind off her work——

HUBERT : You seem to have succeeded.

DAN (*smiling at him, then catching* MRS. BRAMSON's *eye*) : I've thought about it a good bit since, I can tell you. Though it's a bit awkward talking about it in front of strangers ; though you all look very nice people ; but it is a *bit* awkward—

HUBERT : I should jolly well think it is awkward.

for a chap! Though of course, never having been
in the same jam myself——

MRS. BRAMSON: I haven't finished with him yet.

HUBERT: In that case I'm going for my stroll....

He makes for the door to the hall.

OLIVIA: You work at the Tallboys, don't you?

DAN: Yes, miss. (*Grinning*) Twenty-four hours a
day, miss.

HUBERT (*coming to* DAN's *left*): Then perhaps
you can tell us something about the female who's
been murdered?

An unaccountable pause. DAN *looks slowly
from* OLIVIA *to* HUBERT, *and back again.*

Well, *can* you tell us? You know there was a
Mrs. Chalfont staying at the Tallboys who went
off one day?

DAN: Yes.

HUBERT: And nobody's seen her since?

DAN: I know.

MRS. BRAMSON: What's she like?

DAN (*to* MRS. BRAMSON): But I thought you said
—or somebody said—something about—a murder?

HUBERT: Oh, we don't *know*, of course, but there
might have been, mightn't there?

DAN (*suddenly effusive*): Yes, there might have
been, yes!

HUBERT: Ever seen her?

DAN: Oh, yes. I used to take cigarettes an' drinks
for her.

MRS. BRAMSON (*impatiently*): What's she *like*?

DAN: What's she like?... (*To* MRS. BRAMSON)
She's...on the tall side. Thin ankles, with one

44

ᵹ' them bracelets on one of 'em. (*Looking at*
OLIVIA) Fair hair——

*A sudden thought seems to arrest him. He
goes on looking at* OLIVIA.

MRS. BRAMSON : Well? Go on!

DAN (*after a pause, in a level voice*): Thin eye-
brows, with white marks, where they was pulled
out...to be in the fashion, you know.... Her
mouth...a bit thin as well, with red stuff painted
round it, to make it look more; you can rub it
off...I suppose. Her neck...rather thick.
Laughs a bit loud; and then it stops. (*After a
pause*) She's...very lively. (*With a quick smile
that dispels the atmosphere he has unaccountably
created*) You can't say I don't keep my eyes
skinned, can you?

HUBERT : I should say you do! A living portrait,
if ever there was one, what? Now——

MRS. BRAMSON (*pointedly*): Weren't you going
for a walk?

HUBERT : So I was, by Jove! Well, I'll charge off.
Bye-bye.

He goes out of the front door.

OLIVIA (*her manner faintly hostile*): You're very
observant.

DAN : Well, the ladies, you know...

MRS. BRAMSON : If he weren't so observant, that
Dora mightn't be in the flummox she is now.

DAN (*cheerfully*): That's true, ma'am.

OLIVIA (*rising*): You don't sound very repentant.

DAN (*as she crosses, stiffly*): Well, what's done's
done's my motto, isn't it?

*She goes into the sun-room. He makes a gri-
mace after her and holds his left hand out, the
thumb pointing downwards.*

MRS. BRAMSON : And what does that mean ?

DAN : She's a nice bit of ice for next summer,
isn't she ?

MRS. BRAMSON : You're a proper one to talk
about next summer, when Dora there'll be up
hill and down dale with a perambulator. Now
look here, young man, immorality——

MRS. TERENCE *comes in from the kitchen.*

MRS. TERENCE : The butcher wants paying. And
'e says there's men ferreting at the bottom of the
garden looking for that Mrs. Chalfont and do
you know about it.

MRS. BRAMSON (*furious*) : Well, they won't ferret
long, not among my pampas grass ! . . . (*Calling*)
Olivia ! . . . Oh, that girl's never there. (*Wheeling
herself furiously towards the kitchen as* MRS.
TERENCE *makes a move to help her*) Leave me
alone. I don't want to be pushed into the nettles
to-day, thank you. . . . (*Shouting loudly as she
disappears into the kitchen*) Come out of my
garden, you ! Come out !

MRS. TERENCE (*looking towards the kitchen as*
DAN *takes the stub from behind his ear and lights
it*) : Won't let me pay the butcher, so I won't
know where she keeps 'er purse ; but I do know,
so put that in your pipe and smoke it !

DAN (*going to her and jabbing her playfully in
the arm*) : They say down at the Tallboys she's
got enough inside of 'er purse, too.

MRS. TERENCE : Well, nobody's seen it open. If *you* 'ave a peep inside, young fellow, you'll go down in 'istory, that's what you'll do.... (*Dan salutes her. She sniffs*) Something's boiling over.

She rushes back into the kitchen as OLIVIA *comes back from the sun-room.*

OLIVIA : Did Mrs. Bramson call me, do you know?

A pause. He surveys her from under drooping lids, rolling his cigarette on his lower lip.

DAN : I'm sorry, I don't know your name.

OLIVIA : Oh....

She senses his insolence, goes self-consciously to the desk and takes out the wool.

DAN : Not much doin' round here for a girl, is there?

No answer.

It is not a very entertaining quarter of the world for a young lady, is it?

He gives it up as a bad job. DORA *comes in from the kitchen.*

DORA (*eagerly*) : What did she... (*confused, seeing* OLIVIA) Oh, beg pardon, miss....

She hurries back into the kitchen. DAN *jerks his head after her with a laugh and looks at* OLIVIA.

OLIVIA (*arranging wool at the table*) : I'm not a snob, but, in case you ever call here again, I'd like to point out that though I'm employed by my aunt, I'm not quite in Dora's position.

DAN : Oh, I hope not.... (*She turns away, confused. He moves to her.*) Though I'll be putting

47

it all right for Dora. I'm going to marry her. And I——

OLIVIA (*coldly*): I don't believe you.

DAN (*after a pause*): You don't like me, do you?

OLIVIA: No.

DAN (*with a smile*): Well, everybody else does!

OLIVIA (*absorbed in her wool-sorting*): Your eyes are set quite wide apart, your hands are quite good.... I don't really know what's wrong with you.

> DAN *looks at his outspread hands. A pause. He breaks it, and goes nearer to her.*

DAN (*persuasively*): You know, I've been looking at you too. You're lonely, aren't you? I could see——

OLIVIA: I'm sorry, it's a waste of time doing your stuff with me. I'm not the type. (*Crossing to the desk and turning suddenly to him*) Are you playing up to Mrs. Bramson?

DAN: Playin' up?

OLIVIA: It crossed my mind for a minute. You stand a pretty poor chance there, you know.

DAN (*after a pause, smiling*): What d'you bet me?

> OLIVIA *turns from him, annoyed, and puts the wool away.*

> MRS. BRAMSON *careers in from the kitchen in her chair.*

MRS. BRAMSON: They say they've got permits to look for tnat silly woman—who are *they,* I'd like to know? If there's anything I hate, it's these men who think they've got authority.

48

OLIVIA : I don't think they're quite as bad as men who think they've got charm.

She goes back into the sun-room. DAN *whistles.*

MRS. BRAMSON : What did she mean by that?

DAN : Well, it's no good her thinkin' *she's* got any, is it?

MRS. BRAMSON (*sternly*) : Now, young man, what about Dora? I——

DAN : Wait a minute.... (*Putting his hat on the table and going to her*) Are you sure you're comfortable like that? Don't you think, Mrs. Bramson, you ought to be facin'...a wee bit more this side, towards the sun more, eh? (*He moves her chair round till she is in the centre of the room, facing the sun-room*) You're looking pale, you know. (*As she stares at him, putting the stub in an ashtray on the table*) I am sorry. Excuse rudeness.... Another thing, Mrs. Bramson—you don't mind me sayin' it, do you?—but you ought to have a rug, you know. This October weather's very treacherous.

MRS. BRAMSON (*blinking*) : Pale? Did you say pale?

DAN : Washed out. (*His wiles fully turned on, but not overdone in the slightest*) The minute I saw you just now, I said to myself, now there's a lady that's got a lot to contend with.

MRS. BRAMSON : Oh.... Well, I have. Nobody knows it better than me.

DAN : No, I'm sure.... Oh, it must be terrible to watch everybody else striding up and down enjoying everything, and to see everybody tasting the fruit——

As she looks at him, appreciation of what he is saying grows visibly in her face.

I'm sorry.... (*Diffidently*) I didn't ha' ought to say that.

MRS. BRAMSON : But it's true ! As true as you are my witness, and nobody else—— (*Pulling herself together*) Now look here, about that girl——

DAN : Excuse me a minute.... (*Examining her throat, like a doctor*) Would you mind sayin' something ?

MRS. BRAMSON (*taken aback*) : What d'you want me to say ?

DAN : Yes....

MRS. BRAMSON : Yes. What ?

DAN : There's a funny twitching in your neck when you talk—very slight, of course—nerves, I expect—— But I hope your doctor knows all about it.... D'you mind if I ask what your ailments are ?

MRS. BRAMSON : ... Hadn't you better sit down ?

DAN (*sitting*) : Thank you.

MRS. BRAMSON : Well, I have the most terrible palpitations. I——

DAN : Palpitations ! (*Whistling.*) But the way you get about !

MRS. BRAMSON : Oh ?

DAN : It's a pretty bad thing to have, you know. D'you know that nine women out of ten in your position'd be just sittin' down givin' way ?

MRS. BRAMSON : Would they ?

DAN : Yes, they would ! I do know, as a matter of fact. I've known people with palpitations. Somebody very close to me.... (*After a pause, soberly*) They're dead now....

MRS. BRAMSON (*startled*) : Oh !

DAN : My mother, as a matter of fact....

With finely controlled emotion, practically indistinguishable from the real thing.

I can just remember her.

MRS. BRAMSON : Oh ?

DAN : She died when I was six. I know that, because my dad died two years before that.

MRS. BRAMSON (*vaguely*) : Oh.

DAN (*studying her*) : As a matter o' fact——

MRS. BRAMSON : Yes ?

DAN : Oh, no, it's a daft thing——

MRS. BRAMSON (*the old tart note creeping back*) : Come along now ! Out with it !

DAN : It's only fancy, I suppose...but...you remind me a bit of her.

MRS. BRAMSON : Of your mother ? (*As he nods simply, her sentimentality stirring*) Oh...

DAN : Have *you* got a son ?

MRS. BRAMSON (*self-pityingly*) : I haven't anybody at all.

DAN : Oh....But I don't like to talk too much about my mother. (*Putting a finger unobtrusively to his eye*) Makes me feel...sort of sad.... (*With a sudden thought*) She had the same eyes very wide apart as you, and—and the same very good hands.

51

MRS. BRAMSON (*looking interestedly at her fingers*): Oh?...And the same palpitations?

DAN: And the same palpitations. You don't mind me talking about your health, do you?

MRS. BRAMSON: No.

DAN: Well, d'you know, you ought to get used to letting *other* people do things for you.

MRS. BRAMSON (*a great truth dawning on her*): Yes!

DAN: You ought to be *very* careful.

MRS. BRAMSON: Yes! (*After a pause, eyeing him as he smiles at her*) You're a funny boy to be a page-boy.

DAN (*shyly*): D'you think so?

MRS. BRAMSON: Well, now I come to talk to you, you seem so much better class—I mean, you know so much of the world——

DAN: I've knocked about a good bit, you know. Never had any advantages, but I always tried to do the right thing.

MRS. BRAMSON (*patronisingly*): I think you deserve better—— (*sharply again*) Talking of the right thing, what about Dora?

DAN (*disarming*): Oh, I know I'm to blame; I'm not much of a chap, but I'd put things straight like a shot if I had any money....But, you see, I work at the Tallboys, get thirty bob a week, with tips—but listen to me botherin' you with my worries and rubbish the state you're in...well!

MRS. BRAMSON: No, I can stand it.

OLIVIA *comes back from the sun-room.*

(*Pursing her lips, reflectively*) I've taken a liking to you.

DAN : Well... (*looking round at* OLIVIA) That's very kind of you, Mrs. Bramson....

MRS. BRAMSON : It's the way you talked about your mother. That's what it was.

DAN : Was it?

OLIVIA (*at the left window*) : Shall I pack these books?

DAN (*going to her with alacrity, taking the parcel from her*) : I'll post them for you.

OLIVIA : Oh....

DAN : I'm passing Shepperley post office on the bike before post time to-morrow morning. With pleasure!

MRS. BRAMSON : Have you got to go back?

DAN : Now? Well, no, not really.... I've finished on duty now I done that errand, and this is my half day.

MRS. BRAMSON (*imperiously*) : Stay to lunch.

DAN (*apparently taken aback, after a look at* OLIVIA) : Well—I don't like to impose myself——

MRS. BRAMSON : In the kitchen, of course.

DAN : Oh, I know——

MRS. BRAMSON : There's plenty of food! Stay to lunch!

DAN : Well—I don't know...all right, so long as you let me help a bit this morning.... Don't you want some string for this? Where's it kep'?

MRS. BRAMSON : That woman knows. In the kitchen somewhere.

DAN : Through here?

He tosses the books on the sofa and hurries into the kitchen. MRS. BRAMSON *holds out her hands and studies them with a new interest.*

MRS. BRAMSON : That boy's got understanding.

OLIVIA : Enough to marry Dora?

MRS. BRAMSON : You ought to learn to be a little less bitter, my dear. Never hook a man if you don't. With him and that Dora, I'm not so sure it wasn't six of one and half a dozen of the other. I know human nature, and, mark my word, that boy's going to do big things.

A scurry in the garden. MRS. TERENCE *rushes in from the front door, madly excited.*

MRS. TERENCE : The paper-boy's at the back gate, and says there's a placard in Shepperley, and it's got "News of the World—Shepperley Mystery" on it !

MRS. BRAMSON : What !

OLIVIA : They've got it in the papers !

MRS. TERENCE : They've got it in the papers ! D'ye want any? (*Beside herself.*)

MRS. BRAMSON : Catch him quick !

MRS. TERENCE : First time I ever 'eard of Shepperley being in print before—hi !

She races out of the front door.

MRS. BRAMSON : Running around the house shouting like a lunatic ! Sensation mad ! Silly woman !

DORA *runs in from kitchen.*

DORA : They've got it in the papers !

MRS. BRAMSON : Go away !

MRS. TERENCE (*off*) : I've bought three !

MRS. BRAMSON (*shouting*) : Be QUIET !

54

MRS. TERENCE *runs back with three Sunday newspapers and gives one to* OLIVIA *and one to* MRS. BRAMSON.

OLIVIA (*sitting left of the table*): I expect it is a bit of an event.

MRS. TERENCE (*leaning over the table, searching in her paper*): 'E says they're sellin' like ninepins——

MRS. BRAMSON (*turning pages over, impatiently*): Where *is* it?...

MRS. TERENCE: Oh, I expect it's nothink after all....

OLIVIA: Here it is.... (*Reading*) "Disappeared mysteriously...woods round the village being searched"...then her description...tall... blonde....

MRS. TERENCE: Blonde? I should think she is. ...I can't find it!

OLIVIA: Here's something..."A keeper in the Shepperley woods was closely questioned late last night, but he had heard nothing, beyond a woman's voice in the woods on the afternoon in question, and a man's voice, probably with her, singing 'Mighty Lak a Rose.' Enquiries are being pursued...."

MRS. BRAMSON: "Mighty Lak a Rose." What rubbish!...

MRS. TERENCE: Oh yes.... It's the 'eadline in this one. (*Humming the tune absently as she reads*) "Don't know what to call you, but you're mighty lak a rose."... Those men have done rummaging in the garden, anyway

MRS. BRAMSON : I must go this minute and have a look at my pampas grass. And if they've damaged it I'll bring an action.

MRS. TERENCE : Fancy Shepperley bein' in print.

MRS. BRAMSON : Wheel me out, and don't talk so much.

MRS. TERENCE (*manœuvring her through the front door*) : I could talk me 'ead off and not talk as much as some people I could mention.

OLIVIA is alone. A pause. She spreads her paper on the table and finds DAN'S *hat under it. She picks it up and looks at it;* DAN *comes in from the kitchen with a ball of tangled string, a cigarette between his lips. He is about to take the books into the kitchen, when he sees her. He crosses to her.*

DAN : Excuse me.... (*Taking the hat from her, cheerfully*) I think I'll hang it in the hall, same as if I was a visitor....

He does so, then takes up the books, sits on the sofa, and begins to unravel the string. A pause.

You don't mind me stayin' and havin' a bit o' lunch ... in the kitchen, do you?

OLIVIA : It's not for me to say. As I told you before, I'm really a servant here.

DAN (*after a pause*) : You're not a very ordinary servant, though, are you?

OLIVIA (*turning over a page*) : N-no....

DAN : Neither am I.

He unpicks a knot, and begins to hum absent-

mindedly. The humming gradually resolves itself into faint singing.

(*Singing*) "I'm a pretty little feller ... everybody knows ..."

OLIVIA *looks up; a thought crosses her mind. She turns her head and looks at him.*

The Curtain begins to fall slowly.

(*Singing, as he intently unravels the string*) "Don't know what to call me—but I'm mighty lak a rose. ..."

THE CURTAIN IS DOWN

ACT II

SCENE I

*An afternoon twelve days later. The weather is
a little duller.*

MRS. BRAMSON *is sitting on the right of the
table in her invalid chair, puzzling out a game
of patience. She has smartened up her appearance in the interval and is wearing purple, and
earrings.* OLIVIA *is sitting opposite her, smoking
a cigarette, a pencil and pad on the table in
front of her; she is pondering and writing. A
portable gramophone on a small table next the
desk is playing the H.M.V. dance record of
"Dames."*

A pause. MRS. BRAMSON *coughs. She coughs
again, and looks at* OLIVIA, *waving her hand
before her, clearing away billows of imaginary
smoke.*

OLIVIA : I'm sorry. Is my cigarette worrying you ?

MRS. BRAMSON (*temper*) : Not at all. I like it !

OLIVIA *stubs out her cigarette with a resigned
look and goes on making notes.* DAN *enters from
the kitchen, keeping time to the music, carrying
a bunch of roses, wearing overalls over flannel
trousers and a brown golf jacket, and smoking.*

*He goes to the fireplace and clumps the roses
into a vase on the mantelpiece, humming the
tune. He crosses to the gramophone, still in
rhythm,* MRS. BRAMSON *keeping time skittishly
with her hands. He turns off the gramophone
and looks over* OLIVIA's *shoulder at what she
is writing.*

DAN (*singing*): "Their home addresses...and
their caresses...linger in my memory of...those
beautiful dames"... (*His hand to his forehead*)
That's me!

OLIVIA *looks at him coldly and continues her
notes.*

MRS. BRAMSON: It won't come out....

DAN *shrugs his shoulders, stands behind* MRS.
BRAMSON's *chair, and studies her play.* OLIVIA
follows his example from her side.

OLIVIA (*pointing to two cards*): Look.

MRS. BRAMSON (*infuriated*): I saw that! Leave
me alone, and don't interfere.

A pause. DAN *makes a quick movement and
puts one card on another.*

(*Pleased and interested, quite unconscious to the
difference in her attitude*) Oh, yes, dear, of
course....

OLIVIA (*as* MRS. BRAMSON *makes a move*): No,
that's a spade.

MRS. BRAMON (*sharply*): No such thing; it's a
club. It's got a wiggle on it.

DAN: They both got wiggles on 'em. (*Pointing
to another card*) This is a club.

MRS. BRAMSON: Oh yes, dear, so it is!

OLIVIA (*writing*): The ironmonger says **there** *were* two extra gallons of paraffin not paid for.

MRS. BRAMSON : And they *won't* be paid for either —not if I have to go to law about it.

A pause. She coughs absently.

DAN : I'm sorry. Is my cigarette worrying you ?

MRS. BRAMSON : No, no, dear.

This has its effect on OLIVIA. DAN *sits on the left of the table, where "East Lynne" is open on the table.*

I'm sick of patience.

DAN (*reading laboriously*): "You old-fashioned child——"

MRS. BRAMSON : What ?

DAN : *East Lynne.*

MRS. BRAMSON : Oh....

DAN (*reading*): "'You old-fashioned child !' retorted Mrs. Vane. 'Why did you not put on your diamonds ?' 'I—did—put on my diamonds,' stammered Lady Isabel. 'But I—took them off again.' 'What on earth for ?'" That's the other lady speaking there——

MRS. BRAMSON : Yes, dear....

DAN : "'What on earth for ?'...'I did not like to be too fine,' answered Lady Isabel, with a laugh—" (*turning over*) "—and a blush. 'They glittered so ! I feared it might be thought I had put them on to look fine.'"

MRS. BRAMSON (*absently*): Good, isn't it ?

DAN (*flicking ash*): Oh, yes, reelistic.... (*Reading*) "'I see you mean to set up among that class of people who pree-tend to dee-spise ornyment,' scornfully ree-marked Mrs. Vane. 'It is the ree-finement of aff-affectation, Lady Isabel——' "

An excited knock at the kitchen door. DORA *enters.* DAN *turns back the page and surveys what he has been reading, scratching his head.*

MRS. BRAMSON (*the old edge to her voice*) : What is it?

DORA : Them men's in the wood again.

MRS. BRAMSON : What men?

DORA : The men lookin' for that Mrs. Chalfont.

A pause. DAN *hums "Dames" under his breath.*

MRS. BRAMSON : You don't mean to tell me they're still at it? But they've been pottering about since...when was that day Mr. Dan left the Tallboys?

DORA (*stressing a little bitterly*) : *Mister* Dan?

DAN (*smiling*) : Ahem!...

DORA : *Mister* Dan first came to work for you, mum, a week last Monday....

MRS. BRAMSON : Well, I think it's a disgrace——

DORA : *I*'ve found something!

DAN'S *humming stops abruptly; he swivels round and looks at* DORA, *his face unseen by the audience.* OLIVIA *and* MRS. BRAMSON *stare at* DORA; *a pause.*

MRS. BRAMSON : *You've* found something?

OLIVIA : What?

DORA (*excited*) : This!

She holds out her left arm and lets fall from her fist the length of a soiled belt. A pause. OLIVIA *puts down her pencil and pad, goes to her, and looks at the belt.*

64

OLIVIA: Yes, of course, it's mine! I missed it last week....

MRS. BRAMSON (*baulked of excitement*): Oh yes, I thought I recognised it.... What nonsense!...

DAN *looks at her, chuckling.*

DORA (*going, dolefully*): I'm ever so disappointed....

She goes into the kitchen. OLIVIA *goes to the armchair by the fireplace.*

MRS. BRAMSON: She'll be joining Scotland Yard next.... Go on, dear.

DAN (*reading*): "'It is the ree-finement of affectation, Lady Isabel——'"

The clock chimes.

(*Clapping his hands, to* MRS. BRAMSON) Ah!

MRS. BRAMSON (*pleased*): Oh, Danny...

He hurries to the medicine cupboard and pours medicine into a spoon. HUBERT *comes in from the front door.*

HUBERT (*eagerly*): Have you heard?

MRS. BRAMSON (*eagerly*): What?

HUBERT: Dora's found a belt!

MRS. BRAMSON (*disappointed again*): Oh...it was Olivia's.

HUBERT: I say, what a shame!...

MRS. BRAMSON: Tch, tch!... All this sensation-mong——

DAN drowns her speech by deftly pouring the spoonful of medicine down her throat. He pushes her chocolate-box towards her, and strides briskly into the hall.

Horrid....

DAN (*taking a soft hat from the rack and putting it on*): Good for you, though, the way you are....

MRS. BRAMSON: Yes, dear.

DAN (*coming into the room, and beginning to take off his overalls*): And now it's time for your walk.... (*Smiling at* OLIVIA) It's all right, I got trousers on.... (*Peeling the overalls over his feet, and tossing them on to the left window-seat*) Listen to me talking about your walk, when you'll be in a chair all the time.... (*Chuckling, to* HUBERT) That's funny, isn't it!... (*Going to* MRS. BRAMSON) Come on, I got your shawl and your rug in the hall....

MRS. BRAMSON (*as he wheels her into the hall*): Have you got my pills?

DAN: I got them in my pocket.

MRS. BRAMSON: And my chocolates?

DAN: I got them in my pocket too. Here's your hat—better put it on yourself.

MRS. BRAMSON: Yes, dear.

DAN: And here's your shawl.

MRS. BRAMSON: It isn't a shawl, it's a cape.

DAN: Well, I don't know, do I? And I carry your rug on my shoulder.... (*To the others*) See you later! Be good!

Shutting the front door, his voice dying as the chair passes the left window.

Down this way to-day....

A pause. HUBERT *and* OLIVIA *look at each other.*

OLIVIA (*suddenly*): What do *you* think of him?

HUBERT (*a little taken aback*): Him? Grannie's white-headed boy, you mean? Oh, he's all right.

(*Heavily.*) A bit slow on the uptake, of course.
I wish he'd occasionally take that fag-end out of
his mouth.

OLIVIA : He does. For *her*.

HUBERT : That's true. That's why he's made such
a hit with her. Funny I haven't been able to
manage it. In two weeks, too ... it's uncanny.

OLIVIA : Uncanny? ... I think it's clever.

HUBERT : You don't think he's a wrong 'un, do
you ?

OLIVIA : What do we know about him ?

HUBERT : Why ... his Christian name——

OLIVIA : And that's all.

HUBERT : He looks pretty honest.

OLIVIA : Looks ? (*After a pause.*) It's rather
frightening to think what a face can hide. ... I
sometimes catch sight of one looking at me.
Careful lips, and blank eyes. ... And then I find
I'm staring at myself in the glass ... and I realise
how successfully I'm hiding the thoughts I know
so well ... and then I know we're all ... strangers.
Windows, with blinds, and behind them ...
secrets. What's behind *his* eyes ? (*After a pause,
with a smile*) You're quite right, it *is* morbid.

HUBERT : D'you think he's a thief or something ?
By Jove, I left my links on the washstand before
lunch——

OLIVIA : He's acting ... every minute of the time.
I know he is ! But he's acting pretty well, because
I don't know *how* I know. ... He's walking about
here all day, and talking a little, and smiling,
and smoking cigarettes. ... Impenetrable ... that's

67

what it is! What's going on—in his mind? What's
he thinking of? (*Vehemently*) He *is* thinking of
something! All the time! What is it?

*DAN enters from the front door and smiles
broadly at them.*

DAN: Anybody seen my lady's pills? It's a matter
of life and death.... I thought *I* had 'em.

HUBERT *chuckles.*

OLIVIA (*after a pause, in a level voice*): Oh, yes.
They're in the top drawer of the desk. I'm so
sorry.

DAN: Thank you.

*He salutes her, goes to the desk, and takes out
the pills. They watch him.*

MRS. BRAMSON (*off*): Danny!

DAN: Oh, yes, here they are....

HUBERT (*to say something*): Is she feeling off
colour again?

DAN (*on his way to the front door*): Off colour?
She's never been on it, man! To hear her go
on you'd think the only thing left is artificial
respiration, *And* chocolates.... (*Laughing, and
calling*) Coming!

He goes, shutting the front door behind him.

HUBERT: No, really you have to laugh!

OLIVIA: But what you've just seen...that's
exactly what I mean! It's acting! He's not being
himself for a minute—it's all put on for our
benefit...don't you see?

HUBERT (*banteringly*): D'you know, I think
you're in love with him.

OLIVIA (*with rather more impatience than is necessary*): Don't be ridiculous.

HUBERT: I was only joking.

OLIVIA: He's common and insolent, and I dislike him intensely.

MRS. TERENCE *comes in from the kitchen.*

MRS. TERENCE: What'll you 'ave for tea, scones or crumpets? Can't make both.

OLIVIA: What d'*you* think of Dan?

MRS. TERENCE: Dan? Oh, 'e's all right. Bit of a mystery.

HUBERT: Oh.

MRS. TERENCE (*shutting the kitchen door and coming into the middle of the room*): Terrible liar, o' course. But then a lot of us are. Told me he used to 'unt to 'ounds and 'ave 'is own pack. Before 'e went up in the world and went as a page-boy, I suppose.

OLIVIA (*to* HUBERT): You see? He wouldn't try that on with us, but couldn't resist it with her.

HUBERT: I wonder how soon the old girl'll get his number?...Oh, but fair play, we're talking about the chap as if he were the most terrible——

MRS. TERENCE: Why, what's 'e done?

HUBERT: Exactly.

OLIVIA: I don't know, but I feel so strongly... Is Dora there?... (*Calling cautiously*) Dora!

MRS. TERENCE: Oh, she won't know anything. She's as 'alf-witted as she's lazy, and that's sayin' a lot. She'd cut 'er nose off to stop the dust-bin smelling sooner than empty it, she would.

DORA *comes in from the kitchen, wiping her hands on her apron.*

DORA : Did somebody say Dora?

OLIVIA : Has Dan said any more about marry‧ing you?

DORA : No. *She* 'asn't brought it up again, either.

OLIVIA : Does he talk to you at all?

DORA (*perplexed*): Oh...only how-do-you-do and beg-your-pardon. I've never really spent any time in 'is company, you see. Except, o' course——

HUBERT : Quite. What's your idea of him?

DORA : Oh.... (*Moving to the centre of the room*) 'E's all right. Takes 'is fun where 'e finds it. And leaves it.... Cracks 'imself up, you know. Pretends 'e doesn't care a twopenny, but always got 'is eye on what you're thinking of 'im...if you know what I mean.

OLIVIA : Yes, I do. That incredible vanity...they always have it. Always.

HUBERT : Who?

A pause.

OLIVIA : Murderers.

A pause. They stare at her.

HUBERT : Good God!...

MRS. TERENCE : D'you mean...this woman they're looking for?

OLIVIA : I'm sure of it.

MRS. TERENCE : But 'es's such a—such a ordinary boy——

OLIVIA : That's just it—and then he's suddenly so...extraordinary. I've felt it ever since I heard him sing that song—I told you——

HUBERT: That "mighty-lak-a-rose" thing, you mean? Oh, but it's a pretty well-known one——
OLIVIA: It's more than that. I've kept on saying to myself: No, murder's a thing we read about in the papers; it isn't real life; it can't touch us. ...But it can. And it's here. All round us. In the forest...in this house. We're...living with it. (*After a pause, rising decisively*) Bring his luggage in here, will you, Mrs. Terence?
MRS. TERENCE (*staggered*): 'Is luggage? (*Recovering, to* DORA) Give me a 'and.

Wide-eyed, she goes into the kitchen, followed by DORA.

HUBERT: I say, this is a bit thick, you know—spying——
OLIVIA (*urgently*): We may never have the house to ourselves again.

She runs to each window and looks out across the forest. MRS. TERENCE *returns carrying luggage: one large and one small suitcase.*

DORA *follows, lugging an old-fashioned thick leather hat-box.*

MRS. TERENCE *places the suitcases on the table;* DORA *plants the hat-box in the middle of the floor.*

MRS. TERENCE (*in a conspiratorial tone*): This is all.
HUBERT: But look here, we can't do this——

OLIVIA *snaps open the lid of the larger suitcase with a jerk.*

A pause. They look, almost afraid. DORA *moves to the back of the table.*

MRS. TERENCE (*as* OLIVIA *lifts it gingerly*): A dirty shirt...

HUBERT: That's all right.

OLIVIA: A clean pair of socks... packet of razor blades...

HUBERT: We shouldn't be doing this—I feel as if I were at school again——

MRS. TERENCE: Singlet...

OLIVIA: Half ticket to Shepperley Palais de Danse...

MRS. TERENCE: Oh, it's a proper 'aunt!

DORA: Oh, 'ere's a pocket-book. With a letter. (*She gives the letter to* MRS. TERENCE *and the pocket-book to* OLIVIA.)

HUBERT: Look here, this is going a bit too far—you can't do this to a chap——

MRS. TERENCE (*taking the letter from the envelope*): Don't be silly, dear, your wife'll do it to you 'undreds of times.... (*Sniffing the note-paper*) Pooh.... (*Reading, as they crane over her shoulder*) "Dear Baby-Face my own..." Signed Lil....

OLIVIA: What awful writing....

MRS. TERENCE (*reading, heavily*): "...Next time you strike Newcastle, O.K. by me, baby...." Ooh!

HUBERT: Just another servant-girl.... Sorry, Dora....

DORA (*lugubriously*): O.K.

OLIVIA (*rummaging in the pocket-book*): Bus ticket to Thorburton, some snaps...

MRS. TERENCE: Look at 'er *bust*!

OLIVIA: Here's a group.... Look, Hubert....

HUBERT *joins her in front of the table.*

HUBERT: This wench is rather fetching.

MRS. TERENCE (*crowding between them*): Look at 'er!... The impudence, 'er being taken in a bathing-suit!...

DORA: He's not in this one, is 'e?

HUBERT (*impressed*): Oh, I say... there *she* is!

MRS. TERENCE ⎫
⎬ Who?
DORA ⎭

HUBERT: The missing female! In front of the tall man.... You remember the photograph of her in the *Mirror*?

DORA: It's awful to think she may be dead. Awful....

MRS. TERENCE: Looks ever so sexy, doesn't she?

DORA: 'Ere's one of a little boy——

OLIVIA: How extraordinary....

HUBERT: What?

OLIVIA: It's himself.

DORA: The little Eton collar.... Oh, dear... ever so sweet, isn't it?

MRS. TERENCE: Now that's what I call a real innocent face....

HUBERT (*going to the centre of the room*): Well, that's that....

OLIVIA: Wait a minute, wasn't there another one? (*Seeing the hat-box*) Oh, yes....

HUBERT (*lifting it on to a chair*): Oh, this; yes....

DORA: Old-fashioned, isn't it?

73

MRS. TERENCE: I should think he got it from a box-room at the Tallboys——

OLIVIA (*puzzled*): But it looks so extraordinary—— (*She gives a sudden gasp.*)

They look at her. She is staring at the box. A pause.

HUBERT: What is it?

OLIVIA: I don't know.... Suppose there is something...inside it?

A pause. They stare at her, fascinated by her thought. The front door bangs. They are electrified into action: but it is too late. It is DAN. *He goes briskly to the table.*

DAN: She wants to sit in the sun now and have a bit of *East Lynne*. Talk about changin' your mind——

He sees the suitcases on the table before him, and is motionless and silent. A pause. The others dare not move. He finally breaks the situation, takes up "East Lynne" from the table, and walks slowly back to the front door. He stops, looks round at HUBERT, *smiles, and comes down to him. His manner is normal—too normal.*

Could I have it back, please? It's the only one I got....

HUBERT: Oh...yes, of course.... (*Handing him the pocket-book.*)

DAN (*taking it*): Thank you very much.

HUBERT: Not at all...I... (*To* OLIVIA) Here, you deal with this. It's beyond me.

DAN (*to him*): Did you see the picture of me when I was a little fellow?

HUBERT: Yes.... Very jolly.

DAN (*turning to* MRS. TERENCE): Did *you*? It was in the inside of my wallet.

MRS. TERENCE: Oh ... was it?

DAN: Yes. Where I should be keeping my money, only any bit of money I have I always keep *on* me. (*Turning to* HUBERT) Safer, don't you think?

HUBERT (*smiling weakly*): Ye-es....

DAN: I only keep one ten-bob note in this wallet, for emergencies.... (*Looking*) That's funny. It's gone.

He looks at HUBERT. *The others look blankly at one another.*

... I expect I dropped it somewhere.... What did you think of the letter?

HUBERT: Letter?

DAN: You got in your hand.

HUBERT: Well, I didn't—er——

DAN: Means well, does Lil; but we had a row. (*Taking back the letter*) She would spy on me. And if there's anythin' I hate, it's spyin'. Don't you agree?

HUBERT: Ye-es.

DAN: I'd sooner have anythin' than a spy. (*To* MRS. TERENCE) Bar a murderer, o' course.

A pause. He is arranging his property in his wallet.

HUBERT (*incredulous*): What—what did you say?

DAN (*turning to him, casually*): Bar a murderer, o' course.

OLIVIA *steps forward.* MRS. TERENCE *steps back from the chair on which the hat-box has been placed.*

OLIVIA (*incisively*): Talking of murder, do you know anything about Mrs. Chalfont's whereabouts at the moment?

DAN *turns to her, and for the first time sees the hat-box. He stands motionless. A pause.*

DAN: Mrs. Who?

OLIVIA: You can't pretend you've never heard of her.

DAN (*turning to* HUBERT, *recovering himself*): Oh, Mrs. *Chalfont's* whereabouts! I thought she said her name was Mrs. Chalfontswear. (*Profusely*) Silly. . . . Swear—about—couldn't think——

OLIVIA: Well?

DAN (*still looking at* HUBERT, *brightly, after a pause*): I've nothin' to go on, but I think she's been . . . murdered.

HUBERT: Oh, you do?

DAN: Yes, I do.

MRS. TERENCE: Who by?

DAN: They say she had several chaps on a string, and—— (*Suddenly*) There was one fellow, a London chap, a bachelor, very citified—with a fair moust—— (*He stares at* HUBERT.)

HUBERT (*touching his moustache, unconsciously*): What are you looking at me for?

DAN: Well . . . you wasn't round these parts the day she bunked, was you?

HUBERT: Yes, I was, as a matter of fact.

DAN (*significantly*): Oh....

MRS. BRAMSON'S VOICE (*calling in the garden*): Danny!

HUBERT (*flustered*): What in God's name are you getting at?

DAN *smiles and shrugs his shoulders regretfully at him, and goes out through the front door.*
OLIVIA *sits at the table.*

MRS. TERENCE (*to* HUBERT, *perplexed*): Are you *sure* you didn't do it, sir?

HUBERT: I'm going out for a breath of air.

He takes his hat and stick as he goes through the hall, and goes out through the front door.

MRS. TERENCE (*to* OLIVIA): You don't still think——

OLIVIA: I won't say any more. I know how silly it sounds.

DORA *runs into the kitchen, snivelling.*

MRS. TERENCE (*to* OLIVIA): The way you worked us all up! Doesn't it all go to show——

She hears DAN *return, and looks round apprehensively. He goes to the table slowly and looks at the two suitcases.*

DAN (*smiling, to* MRS. TERENCE): Would you mind please givin' me a hand with the tidyin' up?... (*Taking up the suitcases*) And carryin' the other one?... (*Going into the kitchen, followed by* MRS. TERENCE *carrying the hat-box*) Looks as if we're goin' on our holidays, doesn't it?...

OLIVIA *is alone for a moment. She stares before*

her, perplexed. DAN *returns. She looks away. He looks at her, his eyes narrowed. A pause. Studying her, he takes from a pocket of his jacket a formidable-looking clasp-knife, unclasps it, and tests the blade casually with his fingers. He glances at the mantelpiece, crosses to it, takes down a stick, and begins to sharpen the end of it.* OLIVIA *watches him. A pause.*

OLIVIA: *Did* you do it?

He whittles at the stick.

DAN: You wouldn't be bad-lookin' without them glasses.

OLIVIA: It doesn't interest me very much what I look like.

DAN: Don't you believe it.... (*Surveying the shavings in the hearth*) Tch!...Clumsy.... (*Looking round, and seeing a newspaper lying on the table*) Ah....

He crosses to the table.

(*Smiling, with the suspicion of a mock-bow*) Excuse me.... (*He unfolds the newspaper on the table and begins to whittle the stick over it.*)

OLIVIA: You're very conceited, aren't you?

DAN (*reassuringly*): Yes....

OLIVIA: And you *are* acting all the time, aren't you?

DAN (*staring at her, as if astonished*): Actin'? Actin' what? (*Leaning over the table, on both arms*) Look at the way I can look you in the eyes. I'll stare you out....

OLIVIA (*staring into his eyes*): I have a theory it's the criminals who *can* look you in the eyes, and the honest people who blush and look away.

DAN (*smiling*): Oh....

OLIVIA (*after a pause, challenging*): It's a very blank look, though, isn't it?

DAN (*smiling*): Is it?

OLIVIA: You *are* acting, aren't you?

DAN (*after a pause, in a whisper, almost joyfully*): Yes!

OLIVIA (*fascinated*): And what are you like when you stop acting?

DAN: I dunno, it's so long since I stopped.

OLIVIA: But when you're alone?

DAN: Then I act more than ever I do.

OLIVIA: Why?

DAN: I dunno; 'cause I like it.... (*Breaking the scene, pulling a chair round to the table*) Now what d'ye say if *I* ask a question or two for a change? (*Sitting in the chair, facing her*) Just for a change.... Why can't you take a bit of an interest in some other body but me?

OLIVIA (*taken aback*): I'm not interested in you. Only you don't talk. That's bound to make people wonder.

DAN: I can talk a lot sometimes. A drop o' drink makes a power o' difference to me. (*Chuckling*) You'd be surprised.... Ah....

He returns to his work.

OLIVIA: I wonder if I would....

DAN: I know you would....

OLIVIA: I think I can diagnose you all right.

DAN: Carry on.

OLIVIA: You haven't any feelings...at all....

79

He looks slowly up at her. She has struck home.

But you live in a world of your own....A world of your own imagination.

DAN: I don't understand so very well, not bein' so very liter-er-airy.

OLIVIA: You follow me perfectly well.

He shrugs his shoulders, laughs, and goes on whittling.

DAN: D'you still think there's been a bit o' dirty work?

OLIVIA: I don't know what to think now. I suppose not.

DAN (*intent on his work, his back to the audience*): Disappointed?

OLIVIA: What on earth do you mean?

DAN: Disappointed?

OLIVIA (*laughing, in spite of herself*): Yes, I suppose I am.

DAN: Why?

OLIVIA (*the tension at last relaxed*): Oh, I don't know....Because nothing much has ever happened to me, and it's a dull day, and it's the depths of the country....I don't know....

A piercing scream from the bottom of the garden. A pause.

MRS. BRAMSON (*shrieking from the other side of the house*): Danny!...Danny!

The clatter of footsteps in the garden. DORA *runs in from the hall, breathless and terrified.*

DORA: They're diggin'...in the rubbish-pit...

OLIVIA: Well?

DORA: There's something sticking out....
OLIVIA: What?
DORA: A hand...Somebody's hand!...**Oh,**
Miss Grayne...somebody's hand....

She runs whimpering into the kitchen, as
OLIVIA *rises and runs to the left window and*
looks out.

MRS. BRAMSON'S VOICE (*calling off*): Danny!

DAN *rises slowly, his back to the audience.*
OLIVIA *turns and suddenly sees him. Horror*
grows in her face.

The blare of music. The lights dim out.

SCENE II

The music plays in darkness for a few bars,
then the curtain rises again. The music fades
away.

Late afternoon, two days later. OLIVIA *is seated*
above the table snipping long cuttings from news-
papers and pasting them into a ledger. A knock
at the front door. She starts nervously. Another
knock. MRS. TERENCE *comes in from the kitchen*
carrying a smoothing-iron.

MRS. TERENCE: If it's them police again, I'll
bash their helmets in with this. If it lands me
three months, I will.
OLIVIA: They're from Scotland Yard, and **they**
don't wear helmets.

MRS. TERENCE : Then they're going to get 'urt....
(*Going into the hall*) I can tell by their looks
what they think. And they better not think it,
neither.

OLIVIA : And what do they think?

MRS. TERENCE (*over her shoulder*) : They think
it's me. I *know* they think it's me.

*She goes into the hall and opens the front
door.*

HUBERT (*outside*) : Good afternoon, Mrs. Terence.

MRS. TERENCE : Oh ... come in, sir. (*Coming back
into the room*) It's a civilian for a change.

She is followed by HUBERT.

HUBERT (*to* OLIVIA) : I say, this is all getting
pretty terrible, isn't it?

OLIVIA : Yes, terrible.

MRS. TERENCE : Oh, terrible, terrible. There's one
word for it; it's terrible. Forty-eight hours since
they found 'er. They'll never get 'im now.

HUBERT : Terrible....

MRS. TERENCE : There was another charabanc
load just after two o'clock. All standin' round
the rubbish-'eap eatin' sandwiches. Sensation,
that's what it is.

OLIVIA : Would you like some food, Hubert?

HUBERT : Well, I——

MRS. TERENCE : They're still looking for the 'ead.

HUBERT (*to* OLIVIA, *with a slight grimace*) : No,
thanks. I had lunch.

MRS. TERENCE : Mangled, she was, mangled....
Did you see your name in the *Express,* sir?

HUBERT: I—er—did catch a glimpse of it, yes.

MRS. TERENCE: Little did you think, sir, when you was digging that pit for my rubbish, eh? 'E may 'ave been *watchin'* you digging it... ooh! I have to sit in my kitchen and think about it.

HUBERT: Then why don't you leave?

MRS. TERENCE (*indignantly*): How can I leave, with the whole village waitin' on me to tell 'em the latest? (*Going towards the kitchen*) I 'eard 'er 'ead must have been off at one stroke. One stroke....

HUBERT: Really.

MRS. TERENCE (*turning at the door*): She wasn't interfered with, though.

She goes into the kitchen.

HUBERT: How they all love it.... How's the old lady bearing up in the old invalid chair, eh?

OLIVIA: She's bursting out of it with health. And loving it more than anybody. This is my latest job—a press-cutting book. There was a picture of her in the *Chronicle* yesterday; she bought twenty-six copies.

HUBERT (*taking his pipe out*): She'll get to believe she did it herself in the end.... Is she in?

OLIVIA: She's gone over to Breakerly to interview a local paper.

HUBERT: The lad pushing the go-cart?... He's the devoted son all right, isn't he?

OLIVIA (*after a pause*): I don't talk to him much.

HUBERT: Nice fellow. I've thought a lot about that prying into his things—pretty bad show, really, you know. (*Going to the left window*) I wonder if they'll ever nab him?

OLIVIA (*with a start*): What do you mean?

HUBERT: The fellow who did it.... Wonder what he's doing now.

OLIVIA: I wonder.

HUBERT: Damn clever job, you know, quietly.... That was a rum touch, finding that broken lipstick in the rubbish-heap.... You know, the fact they still have no idea where this woman's head is——

OLIVIA (*convulsively*): Don't....

HUBERT: Sorry.

OLIVIA (*after a pause*): It's a bit of a strain.

HUBERT (*earnestly*): Then why don't you leave?

OLIVIA: I—I couldn't afford it.

HUBERT: But you *could*, if you married me! Now, look here—— (*Going to her*) You said you'd tell me to-day. So here I am—er—popping the question again. There's nothing much to add, except to go over the old ground again, and say that I'm not what you'd call a terribly brainy chap, but I am straight.

OLIVIA: Yes, I know.

HUBERT: Though, again, I'm not the sort that gets into corners with a pipe and never opens his mouth from one blessed year's end to the other. I can talk.

OLIVIA: Yes, you can.

HUBERT: An all-round chap, really—that's me.

OLIVIA: Yes.

HUBERT: Well?

OLIVIA : I'm sorry, Hubert, but I can't.

HUBERT : You can't? But you told me that day we might make a go of it, or words to that effect——

OLIVIA : I've thought it over since then, and I'm afraid I can't.

A pause.

HUBERT : What's changed you?

OLIVIA : Nothing's changed me, Hubert. I've just thought the matter over, that's all.

A pause. He crosses towards the fireplace.

HUBERT : Is it another man?

OLIVIA (*startled*) : Don't be silly. (*Collecting herself*) What man could I possibly meet, cooped up here?

HUBERT : Sorry. Can't be helped. Sorry.

DAN (*in the garden*) : There we are.—Nice outing, eh——

OLIVIA : So am I.

The front door opens and DAN *wheels in* MRS. BRAMSON. *He is as serene as ever, but more animated than before. He is dressed the same as in the previous scene, and is smoking his usual cigarette.* HUBERT *sits at the table.*

DAN (*hanging up her rug in the hall*) : Back home again.—I put your gloves away——

MRS. BRAMSON (*as he wheels her in*) : I feel dead. (*To* HUBERT) Oh, it's you.... I feel dead.

DAN (*sitting beside her on the sofa, full of high spirits*) : Don't you be a silly old 'oman, you look as pretty as a picture—strawberries and cream in your face, and not a day over forty;

85

and when I've made you a nice cup of tea you'll be twenty-five in the sun and eighteen with your back to the light, so you think yourself lucky!

MRS. BRAMSON (*as he digs her in the side*): Oh, Danny, you are a terror! (*To the others*) He's been at me like this all the way. I must say it keeps me alive.

DAN (*as she hands him her hat and cape*): But you feel dead. I get you.

MRS. BRAMSON (*kittenish*): Oh, you caution! You'll be the death of me!

DAN (*wagging his finger at her*): Ah-ha! (*Hanging up her things in the hall*) Now what'd you like a drop of in your tea—gin, whisky, liqueur, brandy, or a nice dollop of sailor's rum, eh?

MRS. BRAMSON: Just listen to him! Now don't make me laugh, dear, because there's always my heart.

DAN (*sitting beside her again*): You've lost your heart, you know you have, to the little feller that pushes your pram—you know you have!

MRS. BRAMSON (*laughing shrilly*): Pram! Well! (*Her laugh cut short*) It's wicked to laugh, with this—this thing all round us.

DAN (*sobering portentously*): I forgot. (*As she shivers*) Not in a draught, are you? (*Shutting the front door and coming down to* HUBERT) D'you remember, Mr. Laurie, me pulling your leg about you havin' done it? Funniest thing out!... Talk about laugh!

MRS. BRAMSON (*fondly*): Tttt!...

DAN (*a glint of mischief in his eyes*): I think I better get the tea before I get into hot water.

He goes towards the kitchen.

OLIVIA: Mrs. Terence is getting the tea.

DAN (*at the door*): She don't make tea like me. I'm an old sailor, Miss Grayne. Don't you forget that.

He goes into the kitchen.

OLIVIA: I'm not interested, I'm afraid.

MRS. BRAMSON (*wheeling herself to the front of the table*): Look here, Olivia, you're downright rude to that boy, and if there's one thing that never gets a woman anywhere, it's rudeness. What have you got against him?

HUBERT: Surely he's got more to say for himself to-day than when I met him before?

MRS. BRAMSON: Oh, he's been in rare spirits all day.

HUBERT: Johnny Walker, judging by the whiff of breath I got just now.

MRS. BRAMSON: Meaning whisky?

HUBERT: Yes.

OLIVIA: I've never heard you make a joke before, Hubert.

HUBERT: Didn't realise it was one till I'd said it. Sorry.

MRS. BRAMSON: It's not a joke; it's a libel.

A knock at the front door.

Come in.

NURSE LIBBY *enters from the front door.*

The boy's a teetotaller.

HUBERT: Sorry; my mistake.

87

NURSE: Good afternoon. Shall I wait for you in your bedroom?

MRS. BRAMSON: Yes. I feel absolutely dead.

NURSE (*turning at the bedroom, eagerly*): Anything new *re* the murder?

HUBERT: I believe her head was cut off at one stroke.

NURSE (*brightly*): Oh, poor thing....

She goes into the bedroom. DAN *returns from the kitchen, carrying a tray of tea and cakes.*

DAN: There you are, fresh as a daisy.—Three lumps, as per usual, and some of the cakes you like——

MRS. BRAMSON (*as he pours out her tea*): Thank you, dear....Let me smell your breath. (*After smelling it*) Clean as a whistle. Smells of peppermints.

OLIVIA: Yes. There were some in the kitchen.

HUBERT: Oh.

MRS. BRAMSON (*to* HUBERT, *as* DAN *pours out two more cups*): So you won't stay to tea, Mr.—er——

HUBERT: Er— (*rising*)—no, thank you....

DAN *sits in* HUBERT'S *chair.*

I think I'll get off before it's dark. Good-bye, Mrs. Bramson. Good-bye, Mr.—er——

DAN (*grinning and saluting*): Dan. Just Dan.

He opens the press-cutting ledger.

HUBERT (*to* OLIVIA): Good-bye.

OLIVIA (*rises*): Good-bye, Hubert. I'm sorry.

DAN *raises his cup as if drinking a toast to* MRS. BRAMSON. *She follows suit.*

HUBERT: Can't be helped....It'll get dark early

to-day, I think. Funny how the evenings draw in this time of year. Good night.

DAN : Good night.

HUBERT (*to* OLIVIA) : Good-bye.

OLIVIA : Good-bye.

She goes to the right window-seat.

MRS. BRAMSON : Johnny Walker, indeed ! Impertinence !

DAN (*drinking tea and scanning press-cuttings*) : Johnny Walker?

MRS. BRAMSON : Never you mind, dear.... Any more of those terrible people called? Reporters? Police?

DAN (*gaily*) : There's a defi-nite fallin' off in attendance to-day. Sunday, I expect.

MRS. BRAMSON : Hush, don't talk like that, dear.

DAN : Sorry, mum.

MRS. BRAMSON : And don't call me "mum" !

DAN : Well, if I can't call you Mrs. Bramson, what can I call you?

MRS. BRAMSON : If you were very good, I might let you call me...mother !

DAN (*mischievously, his hand to his forehead*) : O.K., mother.

MRS. BRAMSON (*joining in his laughter*) : Oh, you are in a mood to-day ! (*Suddenly, imperiously*) I want to be read to now.

DAN (*crossing to the desk, in mock resignation*)·: Your servant, mother o' mine.... What'll you have? *The Channings? The Red Court Farm?*

MRS. BRAMSON : I'm tired of them.

DAN: Well...oh! (*Taking a large Bible from the top of the desk*) What about the Bible?

MRS. BRAMSON: The Bible?

DAN: It's Sunday, you know. I was brought up on it!

MRS. BRAMSON: So was I...*East Lynne's* nice, though.

DAN: Not as nice as the Bible.

MRS. BRAMSON (*doubtfully*): All right, dear; makes a nice change....Not that I don't often dip into it.

DAN: I'm sure you do. (*Blowing the dust off the book*) Now where'll I read?

MRS. BRAMSON (*unenthusiastic*): At random's nice, don't you think, dear?

DAN: At random....Yes....

MRS. BRAMSON: The Old Testament.

DAN (*turning over leaves thoughtfully*): At random in the Old Testament's a bit risky, don't you think so?

MRS. TERENCE *comes in from the kitchen.*

MRS. TERENCE (*to* MRS. BRAMSON): The paper-boy's at the back door and says you're in the *News of the World* again.

MRS. BRAMSON (*interested*): Oh!... (*Simulating indifference*) That horrible boy again, when the one thing I want is to blot the whole thing out of my mind.

MRS. TERENCE: 'Ow many copies d'you want?

MRS. BRAMSON: Get three.

MRS. TERENCE: *And* 'e says there's a placard in Shepperley with your name on it.

MRS. BRAMSON : What does it say?

MRS. TERENCE : "Mrs. Bramson Talks."

She goes back towards the kitchen.

MRS. BRAMSON : Oh. (*As* MRS. TERENCE *reaches the kitchen door*) Go at once into Shepperley and order some. At once!

MRS. TERENCE : Can't be done.

MRS. BRAMSON : Can't be done? What d'you mean, can't be done? It's a scandal. What are you paid for?

MRS. TERENCE (*coming back, furious*) : I'm not paid! And 'aven't been for two weeks! And I'm not coming to-morrow unless I am! Put that in your copybook and blot it.

She goes back into the kitchen, banging the door.

MRS. BRAMSON : Isn't paid? Is she mad? (*To* OLIVIA) Are you mad? Why don't you pay her?

OLIVIA (*coming down*) : Because you don't give me the money to do it with.

MRS. BRAMSON : I— (*fumbling at her bodice*)— wheel me over to that cupboard.

OLIVIA *is about to do so, when she catches* DAN's *eye.*

OLIVIA (*to* DAN, *pointedly*) : Perhaps *you'd* go into the kitchen and get the paper from Mrs. Terence?

DAN (*after a second's pause, with a laugh*) : Of course I will, madam! Anythin' you say! Anythin' you say!

He careers into the kitchen, still carrying the Bible. MRS. BRAMSON *has fished up two keys on the end of a long black tape.* OLIVIA *wheels her over to the cupboard above the fireplace.*

OLIVIA: If you give me the key, I'll get it for you.

MRS. BRAMSON: No fear!

She unlocks the cupboard; it turns out to be a small but very substantial safe.

(*Unlocking the safe, muttering to herself*) Won't go into Shepperley, indeed . . . never heard of such impertinence. . . .

She takes out a cash-box from among some deeds, unlocks it with the smaller key, and takes out a mass of five-pound and pound notes. The way these servants—what are you staring at?

OLIVIA: Isn't it rather a lot of money to have in the house?

MRS. BRAMSON: "Put not your trust in banks" is my motto, and always will be.

OLIVIA: But that's hundreds of pounds! It——

MRS. BRAMSON (*handing her two notes*): D'you wonder I wouldn't let you have the key?

OLIVIA: Has . . . anybody else asked you for it?

MRS. BRAMSON (*locking the cash-box and putting it back in the safe*): I wouldn't let a soul touch it. Not a soul. Not even Danny.

She snaps the safe, locks it, and slips the keys back into her bosom.

OLIVIA: Has *he* asked you for it?

MRS. BRAMSON: It's enough to have those policemen prying, you forward girl, without——

OLIVIA (*urgently*): Please! Has he?

MRS. BRAMSON : Well, he did offer to fetch some money yesterday for the dairy. But I wouldn't give him the key! Oh, no!

OLIVIA : Why?

MRS. BRAMSON : Do I want to see him waylaid and attacked, and my key stolen? Oh, no, I told him, that key stays on me——

OLIVIA : Did he—know how much money there is in there?

MRS. BRAMSON : I told him! Do you wonder I stick to the key, I said—what *is* the matter with you, all these questions?

OLIVIA : Oh, it's no use——

She goes to the armchair below the fireplace and sits in it. DAN *returns from the kitchen, with a copy of the "News of the World," the Bible tucked under his arm, a cigarette stub between his lips.*

DAN : He says they're sellin' like hot cakes! (*Handing the paper to* MRS. BRAMSON) There you are, I've found the place for you—whole page, headlines an' all....

MRS. BRAMSON : Oh, yes....

DAN *stands with one knee on the sofa, and turns over the pages of his Bible.*

(*Reading breathlessly, her back to the fireplace*) "...The Victim's Past"...with another picture of me underneath! (*Looking closer, dashed*) Oh, taken at Tonbridge the year before the war; really it isn't right.... (*To* OLIVIA, *savouring it*) "The Bungalow of Death!...Gruesome finds. ...Fiendish murderer still at large.... The

enigma of the missing head...where is it buried?"...Oh, yes! (*She goes on reading silently
to herself.*)

DAN (*suddenly, in a clear voice*): "...Blessed
is the man...that walketh not in the counsel
of the ungodly...nor standeth in the way of
sinners...nor sitteth in the seat of the scornful...."

MRS. BRAMSON (*impatiently*): Oh, the print's too
small....

DAN (*firmly*): Shall I read it to you?

MRS. BRAMSON: Yes, dear, do....

*He shuts the Bible with a bang, throws it on
the sofa, and takes the paper from her.* OLIVIA
*watches him intently; he smiles at her slowly
and brazenly as he shakes out the paper.*

DAN (*reading laboriously*): "...The murderer
committed the crime in the forest most—in the
forest, most likely strippin' beforehand——"

DORA *comes in from the kitchen, and stands at
the door, arrested by his reading. She is dressed
in Sunday best.*

(*reading*) "...and cleansin' himself afterwards
in the forest lake——"

MRS. BRAMSON: Tch! tch!

DAN (*reading*): "...He buried the body shallow
in the open pit, cunnin'ly chancin' it bein' filled,
which it was next day, the eleventh——" (*Nodding at* OLIVIA) That was the day 'fore I come
here....

MRS. BRAMSON: So it was....

DAN (*reading*): "The body was nude. Attempts

94

had been made to...turn to foot of next column...." (*Doing so*) "Attempts had been made to...era—eradicate fingerprints with a knife...." (*Far away, the tolling of village bells. Reading*) "...The head was severed by a skilled person, possibly a butcher. The murderer——" (*He stops suddenly, raises his head, smiles, takes the cigarette stub, puts it behind his ear, and listens.*)

OLIVIA : What's the matter?

MRS. BRAMSON : Can you hear something? Oh, I'm scared....

DAN : I forgot it was Sunday.... They're goin' to church in the villages. All got up in their Sunday best, with prayer-books, and the organ playin', and the windows shinin'. Shinin' on holy things, because holy things isn't afraid of the daylight.

MRS. BRAMSON : But, Danny, what on earth are you——

DAN (*quelling her*) : But all the time the daylight's movin' over the floor, and by the end of the sermon the air in the church is turnin' grey.... And people isn't able to think of holy things so much no more, only of the terrible things that's goin' on outside, that everybody's readin' about in the papers! (*Looking at* OLIVIA) Because they know that though it's still daylight, and everythin's or'nary and quiet...to-day will be the same as all the other days, and come to an end, and it'll be night.... (*After a pause, coming to earth again with a laugh at the others,*

95

throwing the newspaper on the sofa) I forgot it
was Sunday!

MRS. BRAMSON (*overawed*): Good gracious...
what's come over you, Danny?

DAN (*with exaggerated animation*): Oh, I
speechify like anything when I'm roused! I used
to go to Sunday school, see, and the thoughts
sort of come into my head. Like as if I was
readin' off a book! (*Slapping his Bible.*)

MRS. BRAMSON: Dear, dear.... You should have
been a preacher. You should!

DAN *laughs loudly and opens the Bible.*

DORA (*going to the table and collecting the tea-
tray*): I never knew 'e 'ad so many words in 'is
'ead....

MRS. BRAMSON (*suddenly*): I want to lie down
now, and be examined.

DAN (*rising*): Anything you say, mother o'
mine.... Will you have your medicine in your
room as well, eh?

MRS. BRAMSON: Yes, dear.... Olivia, you *never*
got a new bottle yesterday!

DAN (*as he wheels her into her bedroom*): I got
it to-day while you were with the chap....
Popped in at the chemist's.

MRS. BRAMSON: Oh, thank you, dear. The one
by the mortuary?... Oh, my back.... Nurse!...

*Her voice is lost in the bedroom. The daylight
begins to fade. The church bells die away.*

DORA: My sister says all this is wearin' me to a
shadow.

OLIVIA: It is trying, isn't it?

DORA : You look that worried, too, Miss **Grayne**.

OLIVIA : Do I?

DORA : As if you was waiting for something to 'appen.

OLIVIA : Oh?

DORA : Like an explosion. A bomb, or something.

OLIVIA (*smiling*): I don't think that's very likely.... (*Lowering her voice*) Have you talked to Dan at all this week?

DORA : Never get the chance. 'E's too busy dancin' attendance on Madame Crocodile....

DAN *comes back from the bedroom, his cigarette stub between his lips.*

(*Going towards the kitchen*) I'm off. You don't catch me 'ere after dark.

DAN : Why, will ye be late for courting?

DORA : If I was, they'd wait for me. Good afternoon, Miss Grayne. Good afternoon...*sir*.

DAN (*winking at* OLIVIA): Are you sure they'd wait?

DORA : You ought to know.

She goes into the kitchen.

DAN *and* OLIVIA *are alone.* DAN *crosses to the sofa with a laugh, humming gaily.*

DAN : "Their home addresses...and their caresses..."

He sits on the end of the sofa.

OLIVIA : You've been drinking, haven't you?

DAN (*after a pause, quizzically*): You don't miss much, do you?

OLIVIA (*significantly*): No.

DAN (*rubbing his hands*): I've been drinking, and I feel fine!... (*Brandishing the Bible*) You wouldn't like another dose of reading?

OLIVIA: I prefer talking.

DAN (*putting down the Bible*): Carry on.

OLIVIA: Asking questions.

DAN (*catching her eye*): Carry on!

He studies his outspread hands.

OLIVIA (*crisply*): Are you sure you were ever a sailor? Are you sure you weren't a butcher?

A pause. He looks at her, slowly, then breaks the look abruptly.

DAN (*rising with a smile and standing against the mantelpiece*): Aw, talkin's daft! *Doin's* the thing!

OLIVIA: You can talk too.

DAN: Aw, yes! D'you hear me just now? She's right, you know, I should ha' been a preacher. I remember, when I was a kid, sittin' in Sunday school—catching my mother's eye where she was sitting by the door, with the sea behind her; and she pointed to the pulpit, and then to me, as if to say, that's the place for you.... (*Far away, pensive*) I never forgot that.

A pause.

OLIVIA: I don't believe a word of it.

DAN: Neither do I, but it sounds wonderful. (*Leaning over her, confidentially*) I never saw my mam, and I never had a dad, and the first thing I remember is... Cardiff Docks. And you're the first 'oman I ever told that, so you can compliment yourself. Or the drink. (*Laughing*) I think it's the drink.

OLIVIA: You *do* live in your imagination, don't you?

DAN (*reassuringly*): Yes.... It's the only way to bear with the awful things you have to do.

OLIVIA: What awful things?

DAN: Well... (*Grinning like a child and going back to the sofa*) Ah-ha!...I haven't had as much to drink as all that! (*Sitting on the sofa*) Ah-ha!...

OLIVIA: You haven't a very high opinion of women, have you?

DAN *makes a gesture with his hands, pointing the thumbs downwards with a decisive movement.*

DAN: Women don't have to be drunk to talk.... You don't talk that much, though; fair play. (*Looking her up and down, insolently*) You're a dark horse, you are.

A pause. She rises abruptly and stands at the fireplace, her back to him. She takes off her spectacles.

Ye know, this isn't the life for you. What is there to it? Tell me that!

OLIVIA (*sombrely*): What is there to it...?

DAN: Yes....

OLIVIA: Getting up at seven, mending my stockings or washing them, having breakfast with a vixenish old woman and spending the rest of the day with her, in a dreary house in the middle of a wood, and going to bed at eleven....

I'm plain, I haven't got any money, I'm shy, and I haven't got any friends.

DAN (*teasing*): Don't you *like* the old lady?

OLIVIA: I could kill her.

A pause. She realises what she has said.

DAN (*with a laugh*): Oh, no, you couldn't!... Not many people have it in them to kill people.... Oh, no!

She looks at him. A pause. He studies the palms of his hands, chuckling to himself.

OLIVIA: And what was there to *your* life at the Tallboys?

DAN: My life? Well.... The day don't start so good, with a lot of stuck-up boots to clean, and a lot of silly high heels all along the passage waitin' for a polish, and a lot of spoons to clean that's been in the mouths of gapin' fools that looks through me as if I was a dirty window hadn't been cleaned for years.... (*Throwing his stub into the fire in a sudden crescendo of fury*) Orders, orders, orders; go here, do this, don't do that, you idiot, open the door for me, get a move on—I was never meant to take orders, never!... Down in the tea-place there's an old white beard wigglin'. "Waiter, my tea's stone cold." (*Furiously*) I'm not a waiter, I'm a millionaire, and everybody's under me!... And just when I think I got a bit o' peace.... (*His head in his hands*) ... there's somebody ... lockin' the bedroom door ... (*raising his head*) ... won't let me get out; talk, talk, talk, won't fork out with no more money, at me, at me, at me, won't

put no clothes on, calls me everythin', lie on the
floor and screams and screams, so nothin' keeps
that mouth shut only... (*A pause.*) It's rainin'
out of the window, and the leaves is off the
trees...oh, Lord...I wish I could hear a bit o'
music... (*smiling, slowly*)...And I do, inside o'
myself! And I have a drop of drink...and everything's fine! (*Excited*) And when it's the
night...

OLIVIA (*with a cry*): Go on!

*A pause. He realises she is there, and turns
slowly and looks at her.*

DAN (*wagging his finger with a sly smile*): Aha!
I'm too fly for you! You'd like to know, wouldn't
you? Aha! Why would you like to know? (*In-
sistently, mischievously*) Why d'you lie awake
...all night?

OLIVIA: Don't!...I'm frightened of you!...

DAN (*triumphantly, rising and facing her, his
back half to the audience*): Why?

OLIVIA (*desperate*): How do you know I lie
awake at night? Shall I tell you why? Because
you're awake yourself! You can't sleep, can
you?... (*Triumphantly, in her turn*) You *can't
sleep*! There's one thing that keeps you awake
...isn't there? One thing you've pushed into the
back of your mind, and you can't do any more
about it, and you never will....And do you
know what it is?...It's a little thing. A box.
Only a box. But it's...rather heavy....

DAN *looks at her. A long pause. He jerks away
with a laugh and sits at the sofa again.*

DAN (*quietly, prosaically*): The way you was going through my letters the other day—that had to make me smile....

His voice dies away. Without warning, as if seeing something in his mind which makes him lose control, he shrieks loudly, clapping his hands over his eyes: then is silent. He recovers slowly and stares at her.

(*After a pause, in a measured voice*) It's the only thing that keeps me awake, mind you! The only thing! (*Earnestly*) But I don't know what to do....You see, nothing worries me, nothing in the world, only...I don't like a pair of eyes staring at me... (*his voice trailing away*)... with no look in them. I don't know what to do...I don't know...

Without warning he bursts into tears. She sits beside him and seems almost about to put her arms about him. He feels she is there, looks into her eyes, grasps her arm, then pulls himself together abruptly.

(*Rising*) But it's the only thing! I live by myself ... (*clapping his chest*)...inside here—and all the rest of you can go hang! *After* I've made a use of you, though! Nothing's going to stop me! I feel fine! I——

BELSIZE *crosses outside.*

A sharp knock at the front door.

She half rises. He motions her to sit again.

(*With his old swagger*) All right! Anybody's there, I'll deal with 'em—I'll manage myself all right! You watch me!

He goes to the front door and opens it.

BELSIZE (*at the door, jovially*): Hello, Dan! How's things?

DAN (*letting him in and shutting the door*): Not so bad....

He brings BELSIZE *into the room.*

BELSIZE (*as* OLIVIA *goes*): Afternoon, Miss Grayne!

OLIVIA (*putting on her spectacles*): How do you do....

She makes an effort to compose herself and hurries across to the sun-room.

BELSIZE'S *attitude is one of slightly exaggerated breeziness:* DAN'S *is one of cheerful naïveté almost as limpid as on his first appearance.*

BELSIZE: Bearing up, eh?

DAN: Yes, sir, bearin' up, you know....

BELSIZE: We haven't scared you all out of the house yet, I see!

DAN: No chance!

BELSIZE: All these blood-curdlers, eh?

DAN: I should say so!

BELSIZE: No more news for me, I suppose?

DAN: No chance!

BELSIZE: Ah...too bad! Mind if I sit down?

DAN: (*pointing to the sofa*): Well, this is the nearest you get to comfort in this house, sir.

BELSIZE: No, thanks, this'll do.... (*Sitting on a chair at the table, and indicating the cuttings*) I see you keep apace of the news?

DAN: I should say so! They can't hardly wait for the latest on the case in this house, sir.

BELSIZE: Ah, well, it's only natural....I got a bit of a funny feeling bottom of my spine myself crossing by the rubbish-heap.

DAN: Well, will you have a cigarette, sir?... (*His hand to his jacket pocket*) Only a Woodbine——

BELSIZE: No, thanks.

DAN (*after a pause*): Would you like to see Mrs. Bramson, sir?

BELSIZE: Oh, plenty of time. How's she bearing up?

DAN: Well, it's been a bit of a shock for her, them finding the remains of the lady at the bottom of her garden, you know.

BELSIZE: The remains of the lady! I wish you wouldn't talk like that. I've seen 'em.

DAN (*looking over his shoulder at the cuttings*): Well, you see, I haven't.

BELSIZE: You know, I don't mind telling you, they reckon the fellow that did this job was a bloodstained clever chap.

DAN (*smiling*): You don't say?

BELSIZE (*casually*): He was blackmailing her, you know.

DAN: Tch! tch! Was he?

BELSIZE: Whoever he was.

DAN: She had a lot of fellows on a string, though, didn't she?

BELSIZE (*guardedly*): That's true.

DAN: Though this one seems to have made a bit more stir than any of the others, don't he?

BELSIZE : Yes. (*Indicating the cuttings*) Regular film star. Made his name.

DAN (*abstractedly*) : If you *can* make your name without nobody knowin' what it is, o' course.

BELSIZE (*slightly piqued*) : Yes, of course.... But I don't reckon he's been as bright as all that.

DAN (*after a slight pause*) : Oh, you don't?

BELSIZE : No! They'll nab him in no time.

DAN : Oh...Mrs. Bramson'll be that relieved. And the whole country besides....

BELSIZE : Look here, Dan, any self-respecting murderer would have taken care to mutilate the body to such a degree that nobody could recognise it—and here we come and identify it first go! (DAN *folds his arms and looks thoughtful.*) Call that clever?...What d'you think?

DAN *catches his eye and crosses to the sofa.*

DAN : Well, sir, I'm a slow thinker, I am, but though it might be clever to leave the lady unide—unide——

BELSIZE : Unidentified.

DAN (*sitting on the edge of the sofa*) : Thank you, sir.... (*Laboriously*) Well, though it be clever to leave the lady unidentified and not be caught ...hasn't it been more clever to leave her *i*dentified...and still not be caught?

BELSIZE : Why didn't you sleep in your bed on the night of the tenth?

A pause. DAN *stiffens almost imperceptibly.*

DAN : What you say?

BELSIZE : Why didn't you sleep in your bed on the night of the murder?

DAN : I did.

BELSIZE (*lighting his pipe*) : You didn't.

DAN : Yes I did. Oh—except for about half an hour—that's right. I couldn't sleep for toffee and I went up the fire-escape—I remember thinkin' about it next day when the woman was missing, and trying to remember if I could think of anything funny——

BELSIZE : What time was that? (*He rises, crosses to the fireplace, and throws his match into it.*)

DAN : Oh, about...oh, you know how you wake up in the night and don't know what time it is....

BELSIZE (*staring at him doubtfully*) : Mmm...

DAN : I could never sleep when I was at sea, neither, sir.

BELSIZE : Mmm. (*Suddenly*) Are you feeling hot?

DAN : No.

BELSIZE : Your shirt's wet through.

DAN (*after a pause*) : I've been sawin' some wood.

BELSIZE : Why didn't you tell us you were having an affair with the deceased woman?

DAN : Affair? What's that?

BELSIZE : Come along, old chap, I'll use a straighter word if it'll help you. But you're stalling. She was seen by two of the maids talking to you in the shrubbery. Well?

A pause. DAN *bursts into tears, but with a difference. His breakdown a few minutes ago was genuine; this is a good performance, very slightly exaggerated.* BELSIZE *watches him dispassionately, his brows knit.*

DAN: Oh, sir...it's been on my conscience...
ever since...

BELSIZE: So you did have an affair with her?

DAN: Oh, no, sir, not that! I avoided her ever
after that day she stopped me, sir!...You see,
sir, a lady stayin' where I was workin', and for
all I knew married, and all the other fellers she'd
been after, and the brazen way she went on at
me....You're only human, aren't you, sir, and
when they asked me about her, I got frightened
to tell about her stopping me....But now you
know about it, sir, it's a weight off my mind, you
wouldn't believe!... (*Rising, after seeming to
pull himself together*) As a matter of fact, sir, it
was the disgust-like of nearly gettin' mixed up
with her that was keepin' me awake at nights.

BELSIZE: I see....You're a bit of a milk-sop,
aren't you?

DAN (*apparently puzzled*): Am I, sir?

BELSIZE: Yes....That'll be all for to-day. I'll let
you off this once.

DAN: I'm that relieved, sir!

BELSIZE (*crossing to the table for his hat*): But
don't try and keep things from the police another time.

DAN: No chance!

BELSIZE: They always find you out, you know.

DAN: Yes, sir. Would you like a cup o' tea, sir?

BELSIZE: No, thanks. I've got another inquiry
in the village.... (*Turning back, with an after-
thought*) Oh, just one thing—might as well just
do it, we're supposed to with all the chaps we're

questioning, matter of form—if you don't mind.
I'll have a quick look through your luggage. Matter of form....

DAN: Oh, yes.

BELSIZE: Where d' you hang out?

DAN (*lonelessly*): Through the kitchen...here,
sir.... First door facin'...

BELSIZE: First door facing——

DAN: You can't miss it.

BELSIZE: I'll find it.

DAN: It's open, I think.

BELSIZE *goes into the kitchen. A pause.* DAN
looks slowly round the room.
(*Turning mechanically to the kitchen door*) You
can't miss it....

*A pause. The noise of something being moved
beyond the kitchen.* DAN *sits on the sofa with a
jerk, looking before him. His fingers beat a
rapid tattoo on the sides of the sofa. He looks at
them, rises convulsively and walks round the
room, grasping chairs and furniture as he goes
round. He returns to the sofa, sits, and begins
the tattoo again. With a sudden wild automatic
movement he beats his closed fists in rapid suc-
cession against the sides of his head.* BELSIZE
returns, carrying the hat-box.

BELSIZE (*crossing and placing the hat-box on the
table*): This one's locked. Have you got the key?

DAN *rises, and takes a step into the middle of
the room. He looks at the hat-box at last.*

DAN (*in a dead voice*): It isn't mine.

BELSIZE: Not yours?

DAN : No.

BELSIZE : Oh ? ... Whose is it, then ?

DAN : I dunno. It isn't mine.

OLIVIA *stands at the sun-room door.*

OLIVIA : I'm sorry, I thought ... Why, inspector, what are you doing with my box ?

BELSIZE : Yours ?

OLIVIA : Yes ! It's got all my letters in it !

BELSIZE : But it was in ...

OLIVIA : Oh, Dan's room used to be the box-room.

BELSIZE : Oh, I see. ...

OLIVIA : I'll keep it in my wardrobe ; it'll be safer there. ...

With sudden feverish resolution, she picks up the box and carries it into the kitchen. DAN *looks the other way as she passes him.*

BELSIZE : I'm very sorry, miss. (*Scratching his head*) I'm afraid I've offended her. ...

DAN (*smiling*) : She'll be all right, sir. ...

BELSIZE : Well, young feller, I'll be off. You might tell the old lady I popped in, and hope she's better.

DAN (*smiling and nodding*) : Thank you, sir. ... Good day, sir.

BELSIZE : Good day.

He goes out through the front door into the twilight, closing it behind him.

DAN : Good day, sir. ...

A pause, DAN *crumples to the floor in a dead faint.*

QUICK CURTAIN

ACT III

SCENE 1

Half an hour later. The light has waned; the fire is lit and throws a red reflection into the room. DAN *is lying on the sofa, eyes closed.* NURSE LIBBY *sits at the end of the sofa holding his pulse.* MRS. TERENCE *stands behind the sofa with a toby jug of water.*

NURSE: There, lovey, you won't be long now.... Ever so much steadier already.... What a bit o' luck me blowin' in to-day!... Tt! tt! Pouring with sweat, the lad is. Whatever's he been up to?

MRS. TERENCE: When I walked in that door and saw 'im lyin' full stretch on that floor everything went topsy-wopsy. (*Pressing the jug to* DAN'S *lips*) It did! The room went round and round....

NURSE (*as* DAN *splutters*): Don't choke 'im, there's a love....

MRS. TERENCE: D'you know what I said to meself when I saw 'im lyin' there?

NURSE: What?

MRS. TERENCE: I said, "That murderer's been at 'im," I said, "and it's the next victim." I did!

NURSE: So you would! Just like the pictures.... 'Old your 'ead up, love....

113

MRS. TERENCE (*as* NURSE LIBBY *supports* DAN's *head*): Got a *nice* face, 'asn't he?

NURSE: Oh, yes!... (*As* DAN's *eyes flicker*) Shh. he's coming to....

DAN *opens his eyes and looks at her.*

Welcome back to the land of the living!

MRS. TERENCE: Thought the murderer'd got you!

A pause. DAN *stares, then sits up abruptly.*

DAN: How long I been like that?

NURSE: We picked you up ten minutes ago, and I'd say it was twenty minutes before that, roughly-like, that you passed away.

MRS. TERENCE: Passed away, don't frighten the boy!... Whatever come over you, dear?

DAN: I dunno. Felt sick, I think. (*Recovering himself*) Say no more about it, eh? Don't like swinging the lead.... (*His head in his hand.*)

MRS. TERENCE: Waiting 'and and foot on Madame Crocodile, enough to wear King Kong out....

NURSE: That's better, eh?

DAN: Is it really getting dark?

MRS. TERENCE: It's a scandal the way the days are drawin' in.... 'Ave another sip——

DAN (*as she makes to give him more water, to* NURSE LIBBY): You haven't such a thing as a nip of brandy?

NURSE (*opening her bag*): Yes, lovey, I nearly gave you a drop just now——

DAN *takes a flask from her and gulps; he takes a second mouthful. He gives it back, shakes himself, and looks before him.*

MRS. TERENCE: Better?

DAN : Yes.... Clears the brain no end.... **Makes** you understand better.... (*His voice growing in vehemence*) Makes you see what a damn silly thing it is to get the wind up about anything. *Do* things ! Get a move on ! Show 'em what you're made of ! Get a move on ! ... Fainting, indeed. ... Proper girl's trick, I'm ashamed of myself.... (*Looking round, quietly*) The light's going.... The daytime's as if it's never been ; it's dead.... (*Seeing the others stare, with a laugh*) Daft, isn't it ?

DORA *brings in an oil lamp from the kitchen ; she is wearing her outdoor clothes. She crosses to the table, strikes a match with her back to the audience and lights the lamp, then the wall lamp. The twilight is dispelled.*

NURSE (*shutting her bag, rising*) : You'll be all right ; a bit light-headed after the fall, I expect. (*Going to the hall*) Well, got an abscess the other side of Turneyfield, *and* a slow puncture. So long, lovey.

DAN (*sitting up*) : So long !

NURSE : Be good, all !

She bustles out of the front door. A pause. DAN *sits looking before him, drumming his fingers on the sofa.*

DORA (*closing the right window-curtains*) : What's the matter with him ?

MRS. TERENCE : Conked out.

DORA : Conked out ? Oh, dear.... D'you **think** 'e see'd something ? I'll tell you what it is !

MRS. TERENCE (*closing the left window-curtains*):
What?

DORA: The monster's lurking again.

Mechanically DAN *takes a box of matches and
a cigarette from his pocket.*

MRS. TERENCE: I'll give you lurk, my girl, look
at the egg on my toby! Why don't you learn to
wash up, instead of walkin' about talking like
three-halfpennyworth of trash?

DORA: I can't wash up properly in that kitchen,
with that light. Them little oil lamps isn't any
good except to set the place on fire.

She goes into the kitchen. DAN *drums his fingers
on the sofa.* MRS. BRAMSON *wheels herself from
the bedroom.*

MRS. BRAMSON: I dropped off. Why didn't somebody wake me? Have I been missing something?

MRS. TERENCE: That Inspector Belsize called.

MRS. BRAMSON (*testily*): Then why didn't somebody wake me? Dan, what did he want?

DAN: Just a friendly call.

MRS. BRAMSON: You seem very far away, dear.
What's the matter with you?...Dan!

DAN: Bit of an 'eadache, that's all.

MRS. BRAMSON: Doesn't make you deaf, though,
dear, does it?

MRS. TERENCE: Now, now, turnin' against the
apple of your eye; can't 'ave that goin' on——

A sharp knock at the front door. DAN *starts up
and goes towards the hall.*

MRS. BRAMSON (*to* MRS. TERENCE): See who it is.

MRS. TERENCE (*at the front door, as* DAN *is about*

to push past her): Oh...it's only the paraffin boy.... (*To the boy outside, taking a can from him*) And you bring stuff on a Saturday night another time.

DAN *is standing behind* MRS. BRAMSON'S *chair.*

MRS. BRAMSON: I should think so——

MRS. TERENCE *comes into the room.* DAN *strikes a match for his cigarette.*

MRS. TERENCE (*with a cry*): Oh! Can't you see this is paraffin? (*She puts the can on the floor just inside the hall.*)

MRS. BRAMSON: You went through my side like a knife——

MRS. TERENCE: If people knew what to do with their money, they'd put electric light in their 'omes 'stead of dangerin' people's lives.

She goes into the kitchen. DAN *stares before him, the match flickering.*

MRS. BRAMSON (*blowing out the match*): You'll burn your fingers! Set yourself on fire! Absentminded!... I woke up all of a cold shiver. Had a terrible dream.

DAN (*mechanically*): What about?

MRS. BRAMSON: Horrors.... I'm freezing. Get me my shawl off my bed, will you, dear?... (*As he does not move*) My shawl, dear!

DAN *starts, collects himself, and smiles his most ingratiating smile.*

DAN: I *am* sorry, mum. In the Land of Nod, I was! Let me see, what was it your highness was after? A shawl? No sooner said than done.... You watch me! One, two, three!

He runs into the bedroom.

MRS. BRAMSON : Silly boy...silly boy....

OLIVIA *comes in quickly from the kitchen. She is dressed to go out and carries a suitcase.* Where are you off to?

OLIVIA : I—I've had a telegram. A friend of mine in London's very ill.

MRS. BRAMSON : What's the matter with her?

OLIVIA : Pneumonia.

MRS. BRAMSON : Where's the telegram?

OLIVIA : I—I threw it away.

MRS. BRAMSON : Where d'you throw it?

OLIVIA : I—I——

MRS. BRAMSON : You haven't had any telegram.

OLIVIA (*impatiently*) : No, I haven't!

MRS. BRAMSON : What's the matter with you?

OLIVIA : I can't stay in this house to-night.

MRS. BRAMSON : Why not?

OLIVIA : I'm frightened.

MRS. BRAMSON : Oh, don't be——

OLIVIA : Listen to me. I've never known before what it was to be terrified. But when I saw to-day beginning to end, and to-night getting nearer and nearer...I felt my finger-tips getting cold. And I knew it was fright...stark fright. I'm not a fool, and I'm not hysterical...but I've been sitting in my room looking at myself in the glass, trying to control myself, telling myself what are real things...and what aren't. I don't know any longer. The day's over. The forest's all round us. Anything may happen....

You shouldn't stay in this house to-night. That's all.

MRS. BRAMSON (*blustering*): It's very silly of you, trying to scare an old woman with a weak heart. What have you got to be frightened of?

OLIVIA: There's been a murder, you know.

MRS. BRAMSON: Nobody's going to murder *you!* Besides, we've got Danny to look after us. He's as strong as an ox, and no silly nerves about him.... What *is* it you're afraid of?

OLIVIA: I——

MRS. BRAMSON: Sly, aren't you?... Where are you staying to-night?

OLIVIA: In Langbury, with Hubert Laurie and his sister.

MRS. BRAMSON: Not too frightened to make arrangements with *him*, eh?

OLIVIA: Arrangements?

MRS. BRAMSON: Well, some people would call it something else.

OLIVIA (*losing her temper*): Oh, won't you see...

MRS. BRAMSON: I'm very annoyed with you. How are you going to get there?

OLIVIA: Walking.

MRS. BRAMSON: Through the forest? Not too frightened for that, I see.

OLIVIA: I'd rather spend to-night in the forest than in this house.

MRS. BRAMSON: That sounds convincing, I must say. Well, you can go, but when you come back, I'm not so sure I shall answer the door. Think that over in the morning.

OLIVIA : The morning?...

DAN'S VOICE (*in the bedroom, singing*): "... their home addresses...and their caresses...linger in my memory of those beautiful dames..."

OLIVIA *listens, holding her breath ; she tries to say something to* MRS. BRAMSON, *and fails. She makes an effort, and runs out of the front door. It bangs behind her.* DAN *comes back from the bedroom, carrying a shawl.*

DAN (*over-casual*): What was that at the door?

MRS. BRAMSON : My niece. Gone for the night, if you please.

DAN : Gone...for the night? (*He stares before him.*)

MRS. BRAMSON : Would you believe it? Says she's frightened....

A pause.

Come along with the shawl, dear. I'm freezing....

DAN (*with a laugh, putting the shawl round her*): Don't know what's up with me——

He goes to the table and looks at a newspaper.
MRS. TERENCE *comes in from the kitchen, her coat on.*

MRS. TERENCE : Well, I must go on me way rejoicin'.

MRS. BRAMSON : Everybody seems to be going. What *is* all this?

MRS. TERENCE : What d'you want for lunch to-morrow?

MRS. BRAMSON : Lunch to-morrow?...Let me see....

DAN : Lunch ? To-morrow ?... (*After a pause*) What about a nice little steak ?

MRS. BRAMSON : A steak, let me see.... Yes, with baked potatoes——

DAN : And a nice roly-poly puddin', the kind you like ?

MRS. BRAMSON : I think so.

MRS. TERENCE : Something light. O.K. Good night.

She goes back into the kitchen. DAN *scans the newspaper casually.*

MRS. BRAMSON (*inquisitive*) : What are you read·ing, dear ?

DAN (*breezily*) : Only the murder again. About the clues that wasn't any good.

MRS. BRAMSON (*suddenly*) : Danny, *d'you* think Olivia's a thief ?

DAN : Shouldn't be surprised.

MRS. BRAMSON : What !

DAN : Her eyes wasn't very wide apart.

MRS. BRAMSON (*working herself up*) : Goodness me...my jewel-box...what a fool I was to let her go--my ear-rings...the double-faced——

She wheels herself furiously into her bedroom.
DORA, *her hat and coat on, comes in from the kitchen in time to see her go.*

DORA : What's up with her ?

DAN (*still at his paper*) : Thinks she's been robbed.

DORA : Oh, is that all.... That's the fourth time this month she's thought that. One of these days something *will* 'appen to her, and will I be pleased? Oh, baby!... Where's Mrs. Terence?

DAN: Gone, I think.

DORA (*frightened*): Oh, law, no! (*Calling*) Mrs. Terence!

MRS. TERENCE (*calling, in the kitchen*): Ye-es!

DORA: You 'aven't gone without me, 'ave you?

MRS. TERENCE (*appearing at the kitchen door, spearing a hatpin into her hat*): Yes, I'm 'alf-way there. What d'you think?

DORA: You did give me a turn! (*Going to the table and taking the box*) I think I'll 'ave a choc. (*Walking towards the hall*) I couldn't 'ave walked a step in those trees all by myself. Coming?

DAN (*suddenly*): I'd have come with you with pleasure, only I'm going the other direction. Payley Hill way.

MRS. TERENCE (*surprised*): *You* going out?

DORA: Oh?

DAN (*in the hall, putting on hat and mackintosh*): Yes. I still feel a bit funny.

MRS. TERENCE: But you can't leave 'er 'ere by herself!

DORA: She'll scream the place down!

DAN (*over-explanatory*): I asked her, this very minute, and she don't seem to mind. You know what she is. Said it'd do me good, and won't hear of me stayin'. It's no good arguin' with her.

DORA *puts the chocolates down on the occasional table. She and* MRS. TERENCE *follow* DAN *into the hall.*

DORA : No good arguin' with her—don't I know it !

MRS. TERENCE : You 'ave a nice long walk while you get the chance ; you wait on 'er too much.... (*Closing the plush curtains so that they are all out of sight*) Ooh, ain't it dark.... Got the torch, Dora ?

DORA : O.K., honey.

MRS. TERENCE : Laws, I'd be frightened goin' off by meself.... Well, we'd best 'urry, Dora.... Good night, Dan. Pity you aren't comin' our way——

DAN'S VOICE : See you in the morning ! Good night !

DORA'S VOICE : O.K. !... Toodle-oo !

The door bangs. A pause.

DAN'S VOICE (*outside the left window*) : Good night !

MRS. TERENCE'S VOICE (*outside the right window*) : Good night !

DORA (*same*) : Good night !

Silence.

MRS. TERENCE (*farther away*) : Good night !

DORA (*same*) : Good night !

MRS. BRAMSON *comes trundling back from the bedroom in her chair.*

MRS. BRAMSON : Good night here, good night there ; anybody'd think it was the night before Judgment Day. What's the matter with... (*Seeing the room is empty*) Talking to myself. Wish people wouldn't walk out of rooms and leave me high and dry. Don't like it. (*She wheels herself round to the table. A pause. She looks round impatiently.*) Where's my chocolates ?...

She looks round again, gets up out of her chair for the first time in the play, walks quite normally across the room to the mantelpiece, sees her chocolates are not there, walks up to the occasional table, and takes up the box.

That girl's been at them again....

She walks back to her chair, carrying the chocolates, and sits in it again. She begins to munch. She suddenly stops, as if she has heard something.

What's that?...

She listens again. A cry is heard far away.

Oh, God.... Danny!

The cry is repeated.

Danny!

The cry is heard a third time.

It's an owl.... Oh, Lord!

She falls back in relief, and eats another chocolate. The clock strikes the half-hour. Silence. The silence gets on her nerves.

(*After a pause, calling softly*) Danny!... (*As there is no answer*) What's the boy doing in that kitchen?

She takes up the newspaper, sees a headline, and puts it down hastily. She sees the Bible on the table, opens it, and turns over pages.

(*After a pause, suddenly*) I've got the jitters. I've got the jitters. I've got the jitters.... (*Calling loudly*) Danny!

She waits; there is complete silence. She rises, walks over to the kitchen door, and flings it wide open.

(*Shouting*) Danny! (*No reply.*) He's gone....
They've all gone....They've left me.... (*Losing
control, beating her hands wildly on her Bible*)
Oh, Lord, help a poor old woman....They've
left me! (*Tottering to the sun-room*) Danny...
where are you?...Danny...I'm going to be
murdered...I'm going to be murdered!...
Danny... (*Her voice rising, until she is shrieking
hysterically*) Danny! Danny! Danny!

*She stops suddenly. Footsteps on the gravel
outside the front door.*

(*In a strangled whisper*) There's something outside...something outside....Oh, heavens....
(*Staggering across to the sofa*) Danny, where are
you? Where are you? There's something outs——

*The front door bangs. She collapses on the
sofa, terrified, her enormous Bible clasped to her
breast.*

Oh, Lord, help me...help me...Oh, Lord, help
me.... (*Muttering, her eyes closed*)...Forgive us
our trespasses...

The curtains are suddenly parted. It is DAN, *a
cigarette between his lips. He stands motionless,
his feet planted apart, holding the curtains.
There is murder in his face. She is afraid to
look, but is forced to at last.*

Danny....Oh....Oh....

DAN (*smiling, suddenly normal and reassuring*):
That's all right....It's only Danny....

MRS. BRAMSON: Thank God... (*Going off into
laughing hysterics*) Ah...ah...ah...

DAN *throws his cigarette away, lays his hat on*

*the occasional table, throws his mackintosh on
the left window-seat, and sits beside her, patting
her, looking round to see no one has heard her
cries.*

I'll never forgive you, never. Oh, my heart....
Oh—oh—oh——

*He runs across to the medicine cupboard and
brings back a brandy bottle and two glasses.*

DAN : Now have a drop of this.... (*As she winces
at the taste*) Go on, do you good.... (*As she
drinks*) I am sorry, I am really.... You see, they
wanted me to see them to the main path, past
the rubbish-heap, see, in case they was frightened.
... Now that's better, isn't it ?

They are seated side by side on the sofa.

MRS. BRAMSON : I don't know yet.... Give me
some more....

*He pours one out for her, and for himself.
They drink.*

All alone, I was.... (*Her face puckering with self
pity*) Just an old woman calling for help ... (*her
voice breaking*) ... and no answer....

DAN (*putting the bottle on the floor beside him*) :
Poor old mum, runnin' about lookin' for
Danny——

MRS. BRAMSON (*sharply*) : I wasn't running about
as much as all that.... Oh, the relief when I saw
your face——

DAN : I bet you wasn't half glad, eh ?

MRS. BRAMSON : You're the only one that understands me, Danny, that's what you are——

DAN (*patting her*) : That's right——

MRS. BRAMSON: I don't have to tell you everything I've been through. I don't have to tell you about my husband, how unkind and ungodly he was—I wouldn't have minded so much him being ungodly, but oh, he *was* unkind.... (*Sipping*) And I don't have to tell *you* how unkind he was. You know. You just know...whatever else I've not been, I was *always* a great one on psychology.

DAN: You was. (*He takes her glass and fills it again and his own.*)

MRS. BRAMSON: I'm glad those other people have gone. Awful screeching common women. Answer back, answer back, answer back.... Isn't it time for my medicine?

He hands her glass back. They both drink. DAN *sits smiling and nodding at her.*

That day you said to me about me reminding you of your mother.... (DAN *slowly begins to roll up his sleeves a little way.*) These poets and rubbishy people can think all they like about their verses and sonnets and such—that girl Olivia writes sonnets—would you believe it—

DAN: Fancy.

MRS. BRAMSON: They can think all they like, that was a beautiful thought. (*Her arm on his shoulder*) And when you think you're just an ignorant boy, it's ...it's startling.

DAN (*with a loud laugh*): That's right.

MRS. BRAMSON: I'll never forget that. Not as long as I live.... (*Trying to stem her tears*) I want a chocolate now.

DAN : Right you are!... (*Placing her glass and his own on the floor and walking briskly to the table*) A nice one with a soft centre, the kind you like.... Why, here's one straight away.... (*He walks slowly to the back of the sofa. In a level voice*) Now shut your eyes... open your mouth...

MRS. BRAMSON (*purring*): Oh, Danny.... You're the only one...

She shuts her eyes. He stands behind her, and puts the chocolate into her mouth. His fingers close slowly and involuntarily over her neck: she feels his touch, and draws both his hands down, giggling, so that his face almost touches hers.

(*Maudlin*) What strong hands they are.... You're a pet, my little chubby-face, my baby-face, my Danny....Am I in a draught?

A pause. DAN *draws his hands slowly away, walks to the back, and shuts the plush curtains.* I've got to take care of myself, haven't I?

DAN (*turning slowly and looking at her*): You have.

He picks up the paraffin can briskly and goes towards the kitchen.

MRS. BRAMSON : What are you——

DAN : Only takin' the paraffin tin in the kitchen.

He goes into the kitchen.

MRS. BRAMSON (*half to herself*): That girl should have carried it in. Anything to annoy me. To-morrow—— (*Turning and seeing that he is gone*) Danny! (*Shrieking suddenly*) Danny!

DAN *runs back from the kitchen.*

DAN : What's the matter?

He looks hastily towards the hall to see no one has heard.

MRS. BRAMSON : Oh, dear, I thought——

DAN (*sitting on the back of the sofa*) : I was only putting the paraffin away. Now—— (*He leans over the sofa, and raises his arm slowly.*)

MRS. BRAMSON (*putting her hand on his arm*) : I think I'll go to bed now.

DAN (*after a pause, dropping his arm*) : O.K.

MRS. BRAMSON : And I'll have my supper-tray in my room. (*Petulantly*) Get me back into my chair, dear, will you?

DAN (*jerkily*) : O.K....

He crosses to the invalid-chair.

MRS. BRAMSON : Has she put the glass by the bed for my teeth?

DAN (*bringing over the chair*) : I put it there myself.

He helps her into the chair and pulls it over towards the bedroom.

MRS. BRAMSON (*suddenly, in the middle of the room*) : I want to be read to now.

DAN (*after a pause of indecision*) : O.K. (*Clapping his hands effusively*) What'll you have? The old *East Lynne*?

MRS. BRAMSON : No, I don't feel like anything sentimental to-night....

DAN (*looking towards the desk*) : What'll you have, then?

MRS. BRAMSON : I think I'd like the Bible.

A pause. He looks at her.

DAN: O.K.

MRS. BRAMSON (*as he goes smartly to the sofa, fetches the Bible, pulls up a chair to the right of her, sits, and looks for the place*): That piece you were reading....It's Sunday....Isn't that nice...all the aches and pains quiet for once...pretty peaceful....

DAN (*reading*): "Blessed is the man that walketh not in the counsel of the ungodly, nor standeth in the way of sinners, nor sitteth in the seat of the scornful...."

MRS. BRAMSON (*drowsily*): You read so nicely, Danny.

DAN: Very kind of you, my lady. (*Reading a little breathlessly*) "But his delight is in the Law of the Lord; and in His law doth he meditate day and night——"

MRS. BRAMSON: Sh!

DAN: What?

MRS. BRAMSON: What's that?

DAN: Can you hear something?

MRS. BRAMSON: Yes! A sort of—thumping noise....

She looks at him suddenly, leans forward, and puts her right hand inside his jacket.

Why, Danny, it's you! It's your heart...beating!

He laughs.

Well! Are you all right, dear?

DAN: Fine. I been running along the path, see.... (*Garrulously*) I been out of training, I suppose; when I was at sea I never missed a day running round the decks, o' course....

MRS. BRAMSON (*sleepily*): Of course.

DAN (*speaking quickly, as if eager to conjure up a vision*): I remember those mornings—on some sea—very misty pale it is, with the sun like breathing silver where he's comin' up across the water, but not blowing on the sea at all...and the sea-gulls standing on the deck-rail looking at themselves in the water on the deck, and only me about and nothing else...

MRS. BRAMSON (*nodding sleepily*): Yes...

DAN: And the sun. Just me and the sun.

MRS. BRAMSON (*nodding*): There's no sun now, dear; it's night!

A pause. He drums his fingers on the Bible.

DAN: Yes...it's night now. (*Reading, feverishly*) "The ungodly are not so, but are like the chaff which the wind driveth away——"

MRS. BRAMSON: I think I'll go to bye-byes.... We'll have the rest to-morrow, shall we? (*Testily*) Help me, dear, help me, you know what I am——

DAN (*drumming his fingers: suddenly, urgently*): Wait a minute...I—I've only got two more verses——

MRS. BRAMSON: Hurry it up, dear. I don't want to wake up in the morning with a nasty cold.

DAN (*reading slowly*): "...Therefore the ungodly shall not stand in the judgment, nor sinners in the congregation of the righteous....For the Lord knoweth the way of the righteous...But the way of the ungodly...shall perish..."

A pause. He shuts the Bible loudly, and lays it on the table. MRS. BRAMSON *can hardly keep awake.*

That's the end.

MRS. BRAMSON : Is it ?... Ah, well, it's been a long day——

DAN : Are you quite comfortable ?

MRS. BRAMSON : A bit achy. Glad to get to bed. Hope that woman's put my bottle in all right. Bet she hasn't——

DAN : Sure you're comfortable ? Wouldn't you like a cushion back of your head ?

MRS. BRAMSON : No, dear, just wheel me——

DAN (*rising*) : I think you'll be more comfortable with a cushion. (*Rising, humming*) "I'm a pretty little feller, everybody knows... dunno what to call me..."

He goes deliberately across, humming, and picks up a large black cushion from the sofa. His hands close on the cushion, and he stands silent a moment. He moves slowly back to the other side of her; he stands looking at her, his back three-quarters to the audience and his face hidden : he is holding the cushion in both hands.

MRS. BRAMSON shakes herself out of sleep and looks at him.

MRS. BRAMSON : What a funny look on your face, dear. Smiling like that.... (*Foolishly*) You look so kind...

He begins to raise the cushion slowly.

So kind... (*Absently*) What are you going to do with that cushion ?...

The lights dim gradually into complete dark-

*ness, and the music grows into a thunderous
crescendo.*

SCENE II

*The music plays a few bars, then dies down
proportionately as the lights come up again.*

*Half an hour later. The scene is the same, with
the same lighting; the room is empty and the
wheel-chair has been removed.*

DAN *comes in from the sun-room, smoking the
stub of a cigarette. He crosses smartly, takes the
bottle and glasses from the floor by the sofa and
places them on the table, pours himself a quick
drink, places the bottle on the floor next the
desk, throws away his stub, takes another cigarette from his pocket, puts it in his mouth, takes
out a box of matches, and lights a match. The
clock chimes. He looks at it, seems to make a
decision, blows out the match, throws the match-
box on the table, takes* MRS. BRAMSON'S *tape and
keys from his trouser pocket, crosses quickly to
the safe by the fireplace, opens it, takes out the
cash-box, sits on the sofa, unlocks the cash-box,
stuffs the keys back into his trousers, opens the
cash-box, takes out the notes, looks at them, de-
lighted, stuffs them into his pocket, hurries into
the sun-room, returns a second later with the
empty invalid chair, plants it in the middle of
the room, picks up the cushion from the floor
above the table, looks at it a moment, arrested,
throws it callously on the invalid chair, hurries*

into the kitchen, returns immediately with the paraffin, sprinkles it freely over the invalid chair, places the can under the table, lifts the paraffin lamp from the table, and is just about to smash it over the invalid chair when there is the sound of a chair falling over in the sun-room. His face inscrutable, he looks towards it. He carries the lamp stealthily to the desk, puts it down, looks round, picks a chair from near the table, and stands at the sun-room door with the chair held high above his head.

The stagger of footsteps; OLIVIA *stands in the doorway to the sun-room. She has been running through the forest; her clothes are wild, her hair has fallen about her shoulders, and she is no longer wearing her spectacles. She looks nearly beautiful. Her manner is quiet, almost dazed. He lowers the chair slowly and sits on the other side of the table. A pause.*

OLIVIA: I've never seen a dead body before.... I climbed through the window and nearly fell over it. Like a sack of potatoes, or something. I thought it was, at first.... And that's murder.

As he looks up at her.

But it's so ordinary.... I came back...

As he lights his cigarette.

...expecting...ha *(laughing hysterically)*...I don't know...and here I find you, smoking a cigarette...you might have been tidying the room for the night. It's so...ordinary.... *(After a pause, with a cry)* Why don't you *say* something!

DAN : I thought you were goin' to stay the night at that feller's.

OLIVIA : I was.

DAN : What d'you come back for?

OLIVIA (*the words pouring out*): To find you out. You've kept me guessing for a fortnight. Guessing hard. I very nearly knew, all the time. But not quite. And now I do know.

DAN : Why was you so keen on finding me out?

OLIVIA (*vehemently, coming to the table*): In the same way any sane, decent-minded human being would want—would want to have you arrested for the monster you are!

DAN (*quietly*): What d'you come back for?

OLIVIA : I...I've told you....

He smiles at her slowly and shakes his head. She sits at the table and closes her eyes.

I got as far as the edge of the wood. I could see the lights in the village....I came back.

She buries her head in her arms. DAN *rises, looks at her a moment regretfully, puts away his cigarette, and stands with both hands over the invalid chair.*

DAN (*casually*): She didn't keep any money anywhere else, did she?

OLIVIA : I've read a lot about evil——

DAN realises his hands are wet with paraffin and wipes them on his trousers.

DAN : Clumsy....

OLIVIA : I never expected to come across it in real life.

DAN (*lightly*) : You didn't ought to read so much. I never got through a book yet.... But I'll read you all right.... (*Crossing to her, leaning over the table, and smiling at her intently*) You haven't had a drop to drink, and yet you feel as if you had. You never knew there was such a secret part inside of you. All that book-learnin' and moral-me-eye here and social-me-eye there —you took that off on the edge of the wood same as if it was an overcoat...and you left it there!

OLIVIA : I hate you. I...hate you!

DAN (*urgently*): And same as anybody out for the first time without their overcoats, you feel as light as air! Same as I feel, sometimes—only I never had no overcoat— (*Excited*) Why—this is my big chance! You're the one I can tell about meself! Oh, I'm sick o' hearin' how clever everybody else is—I want to tell 'em how clever *I* am for a change!...Money I'm goin' to have, and people doin' what they're told, and *me* tellin' them to do it! There was a 'oman at the Tallboys, wasn't there? She wouldn't be told, would she? She thought she was up 'gainst a soft fellow in a uniform, didn't she? She never knew it was *me* she was dealin' with— (*striking his chest in a paroxysm of elation*)—*me*! And this old girl treatin' me like a son 'cause I made her think she was a chronic invalid—ha! She's been more use to me to-night (*tapping the notes in his jacket pocket, smartly*) than she has to any other body all her life. Stupid, that's what people are ...stupid. If those two hadna' been stupid they might be breathin' now ; you're not stupid ; that's why I'm talkin' to you. (*With exaggerated self-possession*) You said just now murder's ordinary. ... Well, it isn't ordinary at all, see? And I'm not an ordinary chap. There's one big difference 'tween me and other fellows that try this game. I'll *never be found out*. 'Cause I don't care a—— (*Snapping his fingers grandly*) The world's goin' to hear from me. That's me. (*Chuckling*) You wait.... (*After a pause*) But you can't wait, can you?

OLIVIA : What do you mean?

DAN : Well, when I say I'll never be found out, what I mean is, no living soul will be able to tell any other living soul about me. (*Beginning to roll up a sleeve, nonchalantly*) Can you think of anybody ... who can go to-morrow ... and tell the police the fire at Forest Corner ... wasn't an accident at all?

OLIVIA : I—I can.

DAN : Oh, no, you can't.

OLIVIA : Why can't I?

DAN : Well, I'm up against a very serious problem, I am. But the answer to it is as simple as pie, to a feller like me, simple as pie ... (*Rolling up the other sleeve a little way*) She isn't going to be the only one ... found to-morrow ... in the fire at Forest Corner.... (*After a pause*) Aren't you frightened? You ought to be! (*Smiling*) Don't you think I'll do it?

OLIVIA : I know you will. I just can't realise it.

DAN : You know, when I told you all that about

137

meself just now, I'd made up my mind then about you. (*Moving slowly after her, round the table, as she steps back towards the window.*) That's what I am, see? I make up me mind to do a thing, and I do it.... You remember that first day when I come in here? I said to meself then, There's a girl that's got her wits about her; she knows a thing or two; different from the others. I was right, wasn't I? You—— (*Stopping abruptly, and looking round the room*) What's that light in here?

OLIVIA : What light?

DAN : There's somebody in this room's holdin' a flashlight.

OLIVIA : It can't be in this room.... It must be a light in the wood.

DAN : It can't be.

A flashlight crosses the window-curtains. OLIVIA *turns and stares at it.*

OLIVIA : Somebody's watching the bungalow....

He looks at her, as if he did not understand.

DAN (*fiercely*): Nobody's watching!... (*He runs to the window. She backs into the corner of the room.*)

I'm the one that watches! They've got no call to watch me! I'll go out and tell them that, an' all! (*Opening the curtains in a frenzy*) I'm the one that watches!

The light crosses the window again. He stares, then claps his hands over his eyes.

(*Backing to the sofa*) Behind them trees. (*Clutching the invalid chair*) Hundreds back of

each tree.... Thousands of eyes. The whole damn
world's on my track!... (*Sitting on the edge of
the sofa, and listening*) What's that?... Like a
big wall fallin' over into the sea.... (*Closing his
hands over his ears convulsively.*)

OLIVIA (*coming down to him*): They mustn't
come in....

DAN (*turning to her*): Yes, but... (*Staring*)
you're lookin' at me as if you never see'd me
before....

OLIVIA: I never have. Nobody has. You've
stopped acting at last. You're real. Frightened.
Like a child. (*Putting her arm about his shoulders*) They mustn't come in....

DAN: But everything's slippin' away. From underneath our feet.... Can't *you* feel it? Starting
slow... and then hundreds of miles an hour....
I'm goin' backwards!... And there's a wind in
my ears, terrible blowin' wind.... Everything's
going past me, like the telegraph-poles.... All
the things I've ever seen... faster and faster...
backwards—back to the day I was born. (*Shrieking*) I can see it coming... the day I was born!
... (*Turning to her, simply*) I'm goin' to die.

A pause.

A knock at the front door.

It's getting cold.

*Another knock, louder. She presses his head
to her.*

OLIVIA: It's all right. You won't die. I'll tell
them I *made* you do it. I'll tell lies—I'll tell——

A third and louder knock at the front door.

She realises she must answer, goes into the hall, opens the front door, and comes back, hiding DAN *from view.*

BELSIZE (*in the hall*): Good evening.... Sorry to pop back like this——

He comes into the room, followed by DORA *and* MRS. TERENCE, *both terrified.*

(*Looking around*) Everything looks all right here.

MRS. TERENCE: I tell you we *did* 'ear her! Plain as plain! And we'd gone near a quarter of a mile——

DORA: Plain as plain——

MRS. TERENCE: Made my blood run cold. "Danny!" she screamed. "Danny, where are you?" she said. She wanted 'im back, she did, to save 'er——

DORA: Because she was bein' murdered. I knew it! I'd never a' run like that if I 'adn't 'eard——

BELSIZE: We'll soon find out who's right.... Now then—— (*As* OLIVIA *steps aside behind the sofa*) Hello, Dan!

DAN (*quietly, rising and standing by the fireplace*): Hello.

BELSIZE (*standing behind the invalid chair*): Second time to-day, eh?...

DAN: That's right.

BELSIZE: How's the old lady?

DAN (*after a pause*): Not so bad, thanks, inspector! Gone to bed, and says she didn't want to be disturbed——

BELSIZE: Smell of paraffin...

DAN (*with a last desperate attempt at bluster*):
You know what she's like, inspector, a bit nervy
these days——

As BELSIZE *goes to the bedroom and flashes a
light into it.*

I'd no sooner got round the corner she screamed
for me—"Danny, Danny, Danny!" she was
screamin'—"Danny," she calls me, a pet name
for Dan, that is——

As BELSIZE *goes into the sun-room.*

(*Rambling on mechanically*) I told her so then.
I said, "It's dangerous, that's what it is, havin'
so much paraffin in the house." That paraffin—
she shouldn't ha' so much paraffin in the
house——

His voice trails away. Silence. BELSIZE *comes
back, his face intent, one hand in coat pocket.
A pause.*

BELSIZE (*to* OLIVIA): What are you doing here?

OLIVIA: I'm concerned in——

DAN (*loudly, decisively, silencing her*): It's all
right. (*Crossing to* BELSIZE *and swaggering des-
perately, in front of the women*) I'm the feller.
Anything I'm concerned in, I run all by myself.
If there's going to be any putting me on a public
platform to answer any questions, I'm going to
do it by myself... (*looking at* OLIVIA)... or not
at all I'll manage myself all right——

BELSIZE: I get you. Like a bit of limelight, eh?

DAN (*smiling*): Well...

BELSIZE (*as if humouring him*): Let's have a
look at your hands, old boy, will you?

With an amused look at OLIVIA, DAN *holds out his hands. Without warning,* BELSIZE *claps a pair of handcuffs over his wrists.* DAN *stares at them a moment, then sits on the sofa and starts to pull at them furiously over his knee. He beats at them wildly, moaning and crying like an animal. He subsides gradually, looks at the others and rises.*

DAN (*muttering, holding his knee*): Hurt meself....

BELSIZE: That's better.... Better come along quietly....

He goes up towards the hall. DAN *follows him, and takes his hat from the occasional table. As he puts it on he catches sight of his face in the mirror.*

(*To the others, crisply, during this*) I've a couple of men outside. I'll send 'em in. See that nothing's disturbed.... Coming, old chap?

DORA: What's 'e doin'?

MRS. TERENCE: He's lookin' at himself in the glass....

A pause.

DAN (*speaking to the mirror*): This is the real thing, my boy. Actin'.... That's what she said, wasn't it? She was right, you know...I've been playin' up to you, haven't I? I showed you a trick or two, didn't I?...But this is the real thing. (*Swaying*) Got a cigarette?... (*Seeing* OLIVIA) You're not goin' to believe what she said? About helpin' me?

BELSIZE (*humouring him*): No. (*Putting a ciga-*

rette between DAN's *lips and lighting it*) **Plenty of women get a bit hysterical about a lad in your position. You'll find 'em queuing up all right when the time comes. Proposals of marriage by the score.**

DAN (*pleased*): Will they?

BELSIZE: Come along——

DAN *turns to follow him.* DORA *is in the way.*

DAN: Oh, yes...I forgot about you.... (*smiling with a curious detached sadness*) Poor little fellow. Poor little chap.... (*Looking round*) You know, I'd like somethin' now I never wanted before. A long walk, all by meself. And just when I can't have it. (*Laughing*) That's contrary, isn't it?

BELSIZE (*sternly*): Coming?

DAN (*looking at* OLIVIA): Just comin'. (*He goes to* OLIVIA, *takes out his cigarette, puts his manacled arms round her, and kisses her suddenly and violently on the mouth. He releases her with an air of bravado, puts back his cigarette, and looks at her*) Well, I'm goin' to be hanged in the end....But they'll get their money's worth at the trial. You wait!

He smiles, and raises his hand to his hat-brim with the old familiar jaunty gesture of farewell. He walks past BELSIZE *and out through the front door.* BELSIZE *follows him. The bang of the front door.* OLIVIA *falls to the sofa.*

The sound of DORA's *sobbing.*

CURTAIN

NIGHT MUST FALL was first presented in London by J. P. Mitchelhill at the Duchess Theatre on May 31st, 1935, with the following cast:

The Lord Chief Justice	ERIC STANLEY
Mrs. Bramson	MAY WHITTY
Olivia Grayne	ANGELA BADDELEY
Hubert Laurie	BASIL RADFORD
Nurse Libby	DOROTHY LANGLEY
Mrs. Terence	KATHLEEN HARRISON
Dora Parkoe	BETTY JARDINE
Inspector Belsize	MATTHEW BOULTON
Dan	EMLYN WILLIAMS

The play produced by MILES MALLESON.

NIGHT MUST FALL

PROPERTY PLOT

ACT I

Papers.
Books.
Mirror.
Novel (East Lynne).
Oil lamp.
Stuffed birds.
Pictures.
Antimacassars.
Wax fruit.
Chiming clock.
Food.
Dishes.
Newspaper (London *Daily Telegraph*).
Pipe.
Box of chocolates.
Paper with poem.
Roses.
Trays.
Vase.
Cup and saucer.
Medicine.
Vase of flowers.

Wool.
Cigarettes.
3 Sunday newspapers (English).
Ball of tangled string.

ACT II

Cigarettes.
Pad and pencil.
Portable gramophone.
Roses.
Playing cards.
Soiled belt.
Pills.
1 large suitcase.
1 small suitcase.
Leather hat box.
Letter.
Pocket book.
Wallet.
Clasp knife.
Stick.
Newspaper clippings.
Ledger.
Scissors.
Paste.
Tray, tea, cakes, sugar.
Spoons.
Cups and saucers.
Bible.
Keys on black tape.

Cash box.
Deeds.
£1 and £5 notes.
Matches.

ACT III

Jug of water.
Bag.
Flask.
Oil lamp.
Can.
Matches.
Shawl.
Mackintosh.
Hat.
Glasses.
Brandy bottle.
Large black cushion.
Flashlight.
Handcuffs.

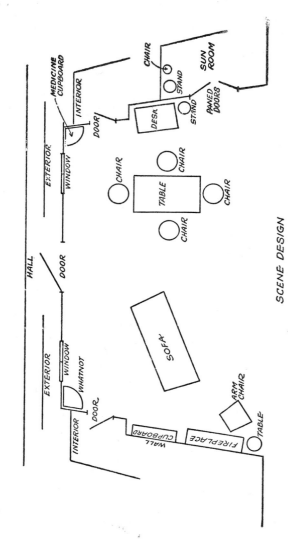

SCENE DESIGN
"NIGHT MUST FALL"

GOODBYE, MY FANCY

Comedy. 3 acts. By Fay Kanin. 8 men, **12 women.**
Interior. Modern costumes.

Here it is! The play that left the Broadway critics wild with
delight and in which the lovely actress, Madeleine Carroll,
gathered such astounding applause. It is the story of a liberal
Congresswoman who returns to her old school as an honorary
visitor. Since her wartime experiences in Europe, she has
devoted herself to the task of acquainting people with the
actual horrors of war. That is why she has brought a docu-
mentary movie with her to be shown to the fresh young
graduates. The movie is considered harsh and improper by the
trustees, however, so Miss Reed has a fight on her hands. The
conflict exposes the president as a spineless and irresolute
figure, instead of the upstanding and outspoken professor with
whom Miss Reed thought she had been in love for so many
years. The disenchantment drives her into the arms of a wartime acquaintance who, as a *Life* photographer, has come to
cover the event. And from there on, it's just one big happy
ending. "There is a hit, a palpable new hit, at the Morosco!
. . . An ardent, adult play with laughter on the surface and,
underneath, a fierce, almost frightening cry for common-sense."
—*N.Y. Journal-American*. It has the sparkle and zing of a
comedy hit."—*Daily Mirror*.

(Royalty, $50.00.)

THE VELVET GLOVE

Comedy. 3 acts. By Rosemary Casey. 5 men, 5
women. Interior. Modern and religious costumes.

A young history professor in a convent school for girls is
about to be dismissed by the harsh Bishop for his modestly liberal views. Happily, the nuns and a kindly old Monsignor rally
around the young instructor, and a very wonderfully portrayed
Mother Superior—who trusts in God but has her own strata-
gems—concocts an innocent plot to change the Bishop's mind.
It is a fascinating comedy as these two pit their wits; and
many a marvelous episode comes and goes before the Bishop
reconsiders. It received bouquets from the critics when the
play appeared on Broadway with Grace George and Walter
Hampden in the leading roles. . . "A pleasant comedy, one of
the year's best."—*Journal American*. "A minor classic."—
World-Telegram. "A comedy of warmth, charm, and humanity
. . . Judging by its enthusiastic reception, the first nighters
agreed with the judges. Among them Katherine Cornell and
Oscar Hammerstein, who chose it."—*Daily Mirror*.

(Royalty, $50.00.)

OUR TOWN

Drama. 3 acts. By Thornton Wilder. 17 males, 7 females, extras. Bare stage. Costumes, 1901.

Winner of the Pulitzer Prize, 1939. The play begins in 1901 in Grover's Corners where the Gibbs and the Webbs are neighbors. During their childhood George Gibbs and Emily Webb are playmates and their lives are inextricably woven together as neighbor's lives are like to be. But as they grow older they pass from this period into a state of romantic but embarrassed interest in one another. And one day, after a slight quarrel, George proposes to Emily in the drug store over an ice cream soda. They are a fine young couple, but their happiness is short-lived, for Emily is taken in death and placed in the village cemetery on a rainy, dreary day. In the most vitally moving scene in the modern theatre is shown the peace and quiet of death which can never be understood by the living. Emily, at first, doesn't understand it, and not until she has gone back to relive her twelfth birthday does she understand that life is a transient fleeting thing and death brings an eternal peace. She takes her place in the graveyard with her friends while George, unable to see beyond his grief, mourns for her.

(Royalty, $25.00.)

TEN LITTLE INDIANS

Mystery. 3 acts. By Agatha Christie. 9 males, 3 females. Interior. Modern costumes.

A superlative type of mystery comedy, first produced at the Broadhurst Theatre in New York. The play takes place in a weird old house on an island. In the house is a mantelpiece on which there are ten little wooden Indians, and above which is an inscription of the nursery rhyme, telling how each little Indian died—until there were none. Ten people are gathered in the house as guests of a mysterious and unseen host. They hear the voice of the host accuse them, each in his turn, of complicity in a murder. Then one by one the guests suffer the different deaths predicted by the voice, and one by one the little wooden Indians topple. With seven down and three to go, the audience is still suspicious and in a fever of excitement. What follows is a tremendously gripping finale, expertly done by one America's top mystery writers.

(Royalty, $50.00.)

THE SKIN OF OUR TEETH

Fantasy. 3 acts. By Thornton Wilder. 4 or 5 important male roles and 4 or 5 important female roles, many small parts and extras, doubling possible. 1 interior, 1 exterior. Various costumes.

Winner of the Pulitzer Prize. A satiric story of the extraordinary adventures of the Antrobus family down through the ages, from the time the great wall of ice creeps over the world to the end of the war—any war. The action jumps from Excelsior, New Jersey, to Atlantic City's Boardwalk and back again, aeons later, to Excelsior. The Antrobuses have survived flood, fire, pestilence, the seven-year locusts, the ice age, the black pox and the double feature, a dozen wars and as many depressions. Ultimately bewitched, befuddled and becalmed, they are the stuff of which heroes are made—heroes and buffoons. They have survived a thousand calamities by the skin of their teeth, and Mr. Wilder's play is a tribute to their indestructibility. The whole play is a testament of faith in humanity.

(Royalty, $50.00.)

"HERE TODAY"

Comedy. 3 acts. By George Oppenheimer. 4 males, 4 females. Interior, exterior. Modern costumes.

First produced in New York at the Ethel Barrymore Theatre by Sam Harris, Mary Hilliard, a brilliant playwright, and Philip Graves, a novelist, were married when they were struggling for success, but the marriage didn't "take" because neither of them would face emotional or financial responsibilities. Now Mary hears that Phil, who is in Nassau, is engaged to Claire Windrew, a society girl, but he is having some trouble with Mrs. Windrew. Claire really is in love with Spencer Grant, a Back Bay lad, who is also arriving in Nassau. So Mary and her wise-cracking collaborator, Stanley, set out to help Phil. With a certain witty perseverance the two of them manage to convince Mrs. Windrew that Phil is probably the catch of the season and that Spencer is a no-good absolutely unworthy of Claire, but they no sooner succeed than Mary realizes she is still in love with Phil. Now they must set about convincing Mrs. Windrew in reverse. By this time Claire has decided she can't stand such carefree people and Phil has decided that he still loves Mary. It is funny, witty, and a constant joy.

(Royalty, $25.00.)

BLITHE SPIRIT

Farce. 3 acts. By Noel Coward. 2 males, 5 females. Interior. Modern costumes.

The smash comedy hit of the London and Broadway stages. The ingenious plot tells how novelist Charles Condomine invites to his country home an eccentric lady medium in order to learn the language of the occult. Neither Charles nor his second wife has any idea that the seance by the medium could summon back Charles' first wife from the beyond. But in she comes, a jealous and mischievous spirit, to torment Charles and break up his marriage. Soon we realize that the first wife is planning a fatal automobile accident for Charles, so that he might join her in a tryst beyond the grave. The scheme misfires and, instead of Charles, the second wife is killed in the accident and passes over to the beyond. There are now two feminine and very blithe spirits, and the trouble they cause Charles provides a ringing climax to a corking good farce. "Hilariously funny, brilliant, clever, and about as cockeyed as a play can be and still stay on the stage."—*N. Y. Journal-American.*

(Royalty, $50.00.)

PARLOR STORY

Comedy. 3 acts. By William McCleery. 6 males, 4 females. Interior. Modern costumes.

This witty and provocative comedy was produced in New York at the Biltmore Theatre. Charles Burnett is a militantly liberal college professor who wants very much to be president of the university. He spurns offers of $20,000 and up as managing editor of a newspaper to teach journalism. His wife is a scheming go-getter who stages his campaign. The office of president is a political appointment, and the governor wants to use it to win votes in the impending election. The upshot of it is that the badgered professor finds his parlor cluttered up with State Troopers, a press tycoon and the Governor. A checker-like game of give and take and double cross ensues. To better his chances for the big college job, the professor is called upon to expel a student, in love with his daughter, for writing a muddled, daring editorial for the campus paper. He refuses, and through a chain of events becomes a strong man, a fighting man, a champion of liberalism in politics. "Some of the most beguiling dialogue of the season."—*N. Y. Times.*

(Royalty, $35.00.)